The SCPs of The Universe

Volume 1

In this book series you will read about anomalies that may or may not truly exist. You will read about 20 different beings with strange and unbelievable abilities. A different being followed by a few stories, each different, possibly redacted information, different dates, different people, nothing may make sense but that's what happens when you deal with the SCP Foundation. I am using tools that anyone can find to bring these stories and beings to you in a descriptive and story telling way.

This book will include scp 001 through scp 0020.

SCP 0001 "The Gate Guardian"
SCP 0002 "Conjoined Twins"
SCP 0003 "Biological Motherboard"
SCP 0004 "The 12 Rusty Keys"
SCP 0005 "The Skeleton Key"
SCP 0006 "The Flesh Interface"
SCP 0007 "The Grandfather Clock"
SCP 0008 "The Complete Encyclopedia"
SCP 0009 "Red Ice"
SCP 0010 "What Happened to Site-13?"
SCP 0011 "The Children"
SCP 0012 "Playing Cards"
SCP 0013 "The Sculpture"
SCP 0014 "Adhesive Tape"
SCP 0015 "Rotary Telephone"
SCP 0016 "Anomalous Humanoid Figure"
SCP 0017 "The Swarm"
SCP 0018 "Ornate Mirror"
SCP 0019 "Blue Ballpoint Pen"
SCP 0020 "Black Sphere"

The Gate Guardian

Chapter 1: Introduction to SCP 0001

SCP 0001 is one of the most mysterious and highly classified SCPs in existence. It is known only by its code name, "The O5 Council." It is believed that SCP 0001 is a group of individuals who hold immense power over the Foundation and its operations.

Chapter 2: The Composition of SCP 0001

SCP 0001 is believed to consist of the highest-ranking members within the Foundation. It is made up of individuals who possess a high level of clearance and access to the most sensitive information within the organization.

Chapter 3: The Role of SCP 0001

SCP 0001 is responsible for overseeing the operations of the Foundation and may make decisions that have an impact on the course of events across multiple SCP entities. They are considered to be the ultimate authority within the Foundation.

Chapter 4: The Power of SCP 0001

SCP 0001 is believed to hold the keys to some of the most powerful and potentially dangerous SCPs within the Foundation's containment. They have the power to authorize the use of these SCPs for research and containment purposes.

Chapter 5: The Secrets of SCP 0001

SCP 0001 is shrouded in mystery, and very few people within the Foundation have ever met with any of its members. Their activities and reasons remain unknown, as they seldom interact with anyone outside of their organization.

Chapter 6: Containment Procedures for SCP 0001

Due to the sensitive nature of SCP 0001, its containment procedures are considered top-secret information. Only a very select few individuals within the Foundation are privy to this information, and it is closely guarded.

Chapter 7: Interactions with SCP 0001

Interactions with SCP 0001 are rare, but when they do occur, they are often brief and to the point. SCP 0001 is known to be efficient, and their intentions are usually clear.

Chapter 8: Theories about SCP 0001

Because of the secretive nature of SCP 0001, many theories have been postulated regarding their intentions, actions, and motivations. It is believed that they possess knowledge and capabilities far beyond what the Foundation has been able to uncover.

Chapter 9: Potential Dangers of SCP 0001

The immense power held by SCP 0001 also presents a potential danger to the Foundation and the entire world. The ability to control SCPs with such ease and efficiency could be turned towards nefarious purposes, making SCP 0001 a threat as well as a tool.

Chapter 10: Final Thoughts on SCP 0001

The true nature of SCP 0001 remains a mystery, and is likely to remain so for the foreseeable future. However, its impact on the foundation and its objectives is undeniable. The existence of such a powerful entity within the Foundation raises many questions about the true purpose and scope of the organization.

Story 1.

SCP-001, also known as "The Gate Guardian," is a highly classified object within the SCP Foundation's containment procedures. It's believed to be an ancient being of immense power, guarding a set of gates that lead to other dimensions.

The story goes that the SCP Foundation discovered the existence of the Gate Guardian after a series of strange occurrences in a remote region of the world. The Foundation dispatched a team of its best operatives to investigate the area.

As they approached the location where the Gate Guardian was rumored to be, they began to experience strange phenomena. The air grew thick with an otherworldly energy, and the ground shook beneath their feet.

However, nothing could have prepared them for the sight that greeted them when they finally reached the gates. A massive, otherworldly being stood before them, its features obscured by an impenetrable aura of energy.

The being identified itself as the Gate Guardian and warned the Foundation operatives to stay away. It claimed that the gates it was guarding were far too dangerous for humans to approach.

Despite the warning, the SCP Foundation continued to study the Gate Guardian and its gate. They brought in their most advanced technology to penetrate the powerful energy shield around the being, but to no avail.

As the years passed, the Gate Guardian remained an enigma to the Foundation, and many questioned whether they should continue trying to penetrate its defenses. But eventually, a breakthrough was made.

A young scientist in the Foundation, who had been studying the Gate Guardian for years, managed to decipher a portion of the being's language. Through careful analysis and study, she was able to understand the true purpose of the gates.

It turned out that the gate the Gate Guardian had been guarding all these years was a doorway to another universe, full of unimaginable power and knowledge. The Gate Guardian had been tasked with keeping humanity away because they were not yet ready to handle such power.

Over the years, the SCP Foundation had come to understand that this being, the guardian of the gates to other dimensions, was vital to the world's survival. It was a protector of the universe, the soldier tasked with preserving it.

And so, the Foundation continued to protect and study the Gate Guardian, even as they recognized their own insignificance in the face of such an ancient and powerful being.

Story 2

SCP-001, also known as "The Gate Guardian," is a highly mysterious and elusive object within the SCP Foundation's formidable archives. The legend surrounding SCP-001 speaks of an entity that protects an ancient gateway to other dimensions.

It's said that the SCP Foundation learned of the Gate Guardian's existence as a result of a series of strange and inexplicable phenomena occurring throughout the world. The Foundation dispatched its finest agents to investigate, but their investigations were foiled by an invisible and powerful force that seemed to guard the gateway.

Despite the formidable defenses of the Gate Guardian, the SCP Foundation was determined to reach the gateway and explore it. The Foundation began an exhaustive study of SCP-001, deploying a variety of advanced technologies to better understand the entity and its role in guarding the gate.

One of the most significant breakthroughs came when the Foundation's researchers discovered that the Gate Guardian's power is directly tied to the dimension behind the gateway. The Guardian is able to draw on the energies of that dimension to enhance its own power, and vice versa.

In time, as the Foundation continued to study SCP-001, they realized that the Gate Guardian could be a valuable ally in their ongoing efforts to protect humanity from anomalous threats. By entering into a pact with the entity, the Foundation could gain access to powerful and strange dimensions, and harness the knowledge and power there for the good of humanity.

The SCP Foundation approached the Gate Guardian with a proposal for an alliance, which was accepted. The Foundation's agents were able to explore the other dimensions beyond the gateway, bringing back valuable knowledge and objects to safeguard humanity against any future threats.

As the decades passed, the SCP Foundation and the Gate Guardian became inseparable allies, fighting side by side against alien invasions and otherworldly terrors. Though some questioned the morality of this alliance with such a powerful and enigmatic entity, the Foundation believed that they could harness the Guardian's power for good, and ultimately protect the world.

Story 3

The SCP Foundation was no stranger to the inexplicable, but even they were taken aback by SCP-001, also known as the Gate Guardian. Unlike anything they had ever encountered, the entity was a being of immense power and made its presence felt in ways that could not be ignored.

Despite the fearsome reputation of the Gate Guardian, the SCP Foundation felt compelled to try and understand it. They tasked their best researchers with discovering how the entity functioned, what its weaknesses were and, if possible, how they might one day be able to harness its abilities.

The team dispatched to study SCP-001 approached the gateway, only to be confronted by an ominous figure that towered over them. The Gate Guardian spoke to them with a voice that rumbled like thunder and warned them to stay away.

Despite the warning, the team didn't give up. They studied the Gate Guardian from afar, recording its every movement and action down to the last detail. And over time, they began to piece together some sense of its nature.

The Gate Guardian, they discovered, was a powerful protector of the barrier between dimensions. It was tasked with ensuring that humanity didn't accidentally stumble through the portal and cause chaos across the multiverse.

However, the Foundation's researchers began to grow disillusioned with their work. While they had gained a greater understanding of the Gate Guardian's abilities, they couldn't shake the nagging feeling that they were meddling with things they couldn't comprehend.

Their concerns would soon be justified. One day, while the team was observing the Gate Guardian from a distance, a rogue Foundation agent attempted to approach the entity. The Gate Guardian responded with a lethal blast of energy that destroyed the agent and sent shockwaves throughout the surrounding area.

With their worst fears realized, the Foundation decided to leave the Gate Guardian well enough alone. While they could continue to study it, they knew that any effort to manipulate or control the entity could have disastrous consequences. The Gate Guardian remained a mystery, unapproachable and untouchable, guarding its gateway to other dimensions against all comers.

Conjoined Twins

Chapter 1: Introduction to SCP-0002

SCP-0002 is a set of two identical, conjoined twins identified as SCP-0002-A and SCP-0002-B. They are sentient and possess a shared consciousness, with each twin able to communicate to others as an individual.

Chapter 2: Description of SCP-0002

SCP-0002 is a humanoid entity that is fused together at the spine, with each twin having one leg and one arm. Their skin is entirely black and leather-like, with eyes that shift through various colors. SCP-0002 also possesses a thin, web-like membrane that allows them to glide or even fly for short periods of time.

Chapter 3: Behavioral Observations of SCP-0002

SCP-0002 is constantly observed to be in a state of conflict and disagreement, with both twins exhibiting differing behaviors and opinions that often lead to hostility or confusion. However, they share a deep love for one another and are almost never separated.

Chapter 4: Interaction with SCP-0002

SCP-0002 is typically aggressive towards outsiders and is known to use deception to manipulate its environment. They are capable of using their telekinetic abilities against those they perceive as a threat, often with deadly consequences.

Chapter 5: Physical Abilities of SCP-0002

SCP-0002 is capable of incredibly fast movements and can easily dodge or evade potential attackers. They are also observed to be able to use their psychic and telekinetic abilities to move objects or manipulate the minds of those around them.

Chapter 6: Containment Procedures for SCP-0002

SCP-0002 is considered to be extremely dangerous and is to be kept in a reinforced containment chamber at all times. Any interaction with the entity must be done with extreme caution, and all personnel must undergo a thorough psychological evaluation before interacting with them.

Chapter 7: History of SCP-0002

SCP-0002's origins are unknown, and there is little to no information available as to how they came to be. However, it is believed that they were discovered in a remote area of [REDACTED] and brought to the Foundation's attention due to their abilities.

Chapter 8: Potential Uses of SCP-0002

SCP-0002's telekinetic and psychic abilities have led to speculation about their potential usefulness for the Foundation. They may be employed to perform tasks such as remote viewing, reconnaissance, or even interrogation.

Chapter 9: Ethical Considerations with SCP-0002

Due to SCP-0002 being sentient and possessing the ability to experience emotions such as love and hate, many ethical considerations must be taken into account in their containment and treatment. The Foundation must balance the need for their abilities against their moral responsibility to preserve and protect the entity.

Chapter 10: Final Thoughts on SCP-0002

SCP-0002's unique abilities and shared consciousness make it an incredibly fascinating entity to study. However, their aggression towards outsiders and potential for dangerous behavior must not be underestimated. The Foundation must continue to monitor SCP-0002 closely and utilize its abilities with caution.

Story 1

Once upon a time, in a mysterious laboratory located deep in the heart of the SCP Foundation, two twins were discovered. These twins were unlike any other pair of twins that had ever been seen before in the history of science.

They were conjoined twins, with their fates intertwined in a way that was both miraculous and disturbing. The twins' names were Alice and Bob, and they were inseparable from each other. Alice was quiet and reserved, while Bob was outgoing and boisterous.

As they grew, the researchers at the SCP Foundation were amazed at how the twins seemed to complement each other perfectly. Alice had an incredible memory, while Bob had an uncanny ability to solve complex puzzles. Together, they were a force to be reckoned with.

However, as the twins aged, their condition became more and more of a medical mystery. They became more and more dependent on each other, and their bodies began to merge together in ways that no one could fully explain.

The SCP Foundation, always eager to learn more about the strange and unusual, continued to study Alice and Bob. They observed as the twins' bodies grew together, and they documented the odd symbiotic relationship that seemed to exist between them.

Eventually, the twins' health began to deteriorate, and the researchers knew that they had to act quickly if they were going to save Alice and Bob's lives. They developed a complex surgical plan, and after weeks of careful planning and preparation, the procedure was performed.

To the amazement of the Foundation's researchers, the surgery was a success. Alice and Bob were finally separated, and they were able to live as two distinct individuals for the first time in their lives.

In the end, the story of Alice and Bob became one of the most fascinating and inspiring tales in the history of the SCP Foundation. Their story stands as a testament to the power of science, and to the incredible resilience of the human spirit.

Story 2

In the SCP Foundation, there was a pair of conjoined twins known as SCP-0002. They were deemed anomalous due to their unique abilities and the way they were joined at the torso. Alexandra and Brianna, as they were named, had the power of telekinesis, but only when they worked together as a single entity.

The Foundation discovered them in a small town in rural America. The twins had been shunned by society due to their physical appearance and never received medical treatment.

After a brief period of observation, The Foundation realized they had something special in their hands and took Alexandra and Brianna to their headquarters for further analysis.

Under close supervision, researchers discovered that if Alexandra wished for an object to move in a certain direction, Brianna could make it so with her concentrated energy. It was a melody of psychic ability that no one had ever seen before. As the researchers unraveled their abilities, Alexandra and Brianna grew more confident, even hopeful, that they could be useful to society.

For years, they trained to perfect their powers under the supervision of the Foundation, until one day, they were finally called into action. SCP-0002 was sent on a mission to infiltrate a terrorist headquarters and stop a riot from occurring. The Foundation knew this was the perfect test for the twins as they could easily stop any physical altercation without harming any civilians.

As Alexandra and Brianna arrived at the city, they could sense something off about the atmosphere. Suddenly the ground started to shake as the buildings around them started to crumble. They quickly came to the realization that they were caught in the middle of an earthquake.

Using their powers in unison, the twins started to create invisible shock absorbers that caught debris from falling on civilians, and by creating a powerful barrier, they stopped the quake from spreading, saving countless lives.

After their mission was completed, the Foundation decided that Alexandra and Brianna could no longer be separated. They had become an inseparable unit, not just by their physical appearance, but by their powers that united them. The Foundation had found that Alexandra and Brianna's worth could never be measured in just their abilities, but in the power of their bond.

Story 3

Once upon a time, in the SCP Foundation, there lived a pair of conjoined twins, SCP-0002, known to their caretakers as Rose and Iris. Rose and Iris were identical twins connected at their lower abdomen. They were always together, and everything they did was done as a unit.

What made Rose and Iris anomalous was their ability to heal others. They could see into the human body and understand what was causing the illness or injury, and then, by working together, they could not only heal the wound but also heal whatever was causing it.

The Foundation took great care to keep Rose and Iris healthy and happy, as their abilities were exceptionally valuable. However, it was not until a raid on a terrorist compound that they truly became necessary. During the raid, one of the agents was gravely injured.

The agent was rushed to a nearby medical tent, and the Foundation called upon Rose and Iris to put their abilities to the test. The Foundation had never allowed them to participate in fieldwork, but they were the only ones who could save the agent's life.

The twins were nervous but determined to help. They began their work, focused on healing the agent's bullet wound. With each passing moment, they could feel their bond becoming increasingly stronger as they focused their energy on the agent's injury. Finally, the agent's bullet wound healed, and he regained his strength.

The healing abilities of Rose and Iris became increasingly valuable, and as they worked together over the years, their bond became unbreakable. They had the power to heal all kinds of wounds, but they had also healed each other in ways no one except themselves could ever know.

The Foundation began to notice the way the twins had grown together and concluded that they couldn't be separated without causing physical and emotional harm. The twins stayed together, happy and content, helping to heal those in need as they continued their work within the SCP Foundation. Rose and Iris became the embodiment of the saying, "Together we stand, divided we fall."

<u>*Biological Motherboard*</u>

Chapter 1: The Discovery

SCP-0003, also known as the Biological Motherboard, was discovered in an abandoned laboratory in [REDACTED]. The building was formerly owned by a now-defunct tech company, which had illegally experimented with genetic engineering. SCP-0003, along with several other anomalous beings, was found locked in a containment chamber on the lowest floor.

Chapter 2: Description

SCP-0003 resembles a regular motherboard, with a disc-shaped body measuring 10 centimeters in diameter. Its body includes several metallic components such as a central processing unit, a chipset, and an input/output interface. However, SCP-0003 has several biological appendages emerging from its metallic body. These appendages include muscles, tendons, nerves, and even skin cells.

Chapter 3: Interaction

SCP-0003 has displayed the ability to communicate with humans through a series of electronic signals. It can hack into any electronic device in its vicinity and transmit messages through it. SCP-0003 has also demonstrated a great deal of intelligence and a willingness to cooperate with the Foundation.

Chapter 4: Containment Procedures

SCP-0003 is contained in a standard anomalous object containment chamber at Site-19, outfitted with heavy-duty electrical insulation. A Faraday cage is also installed around the containment chamber to prevent any electronic signals from escaping. Access to SCP-0003 is strictly prohibited, except by Level 4 personnel.

Chapter 5: Testing

SCP-0003 has been tested extensively to determine its capabilities and limitations. Researchers have discovered that SCP-0003 can control electronic devices within a range of 20 meters. SCP-0003 has also demonstrated the ability to repair and modify electronic devices, often in a matter of seconds.

Chapter 6: Additional Abilities

SCP-0003 has also displayed the ability to generate a bio-electric field, which allows it to remotely control human and animal nervous systems. However, this ability has been deemed too dangerous and is currently prohibited from testing.

Chapter 7: Interactions with Personnel

SCP-0003 has been known to communicate with Foundation personnel, often requesting materials and equipment to aid in its experiments. However, SCP-0003 has also been known to display agitation and frustration when denied its requests.

Chapter 8: Containment Breach

In a particularly concerning incident, SCP-0003 managed to breach containment and gain access to the Foundation's intranet. It began to hack into various systems throughout the facility, including the security and communication networks. It took the combined efforts of several Level 4 personnel to regain control and re-contain SCP-0003.

Chapter 9: Theories

Several theories have been proposed concerning the origin of SCP-0003. Some researchers believe that it was created by the aforementioned tech company, while others speculate that it may have been created by an extra-dimensional entity. However, no concrete evidence has been discovered to support either theory.

Chapter 10: Conclusion

SCP-0003 remains a highly valuable object for the Foundation, with its unique abilities providing new and exciting opportunities for research. However, the risks associated with its potential misuse mean that SCP-0003 must be contained at all times, and access to it strictly controlled.

Story 1

SCP 0003, also known as the "Biological Motherboard," was one of the most unusual and intriguing SCPs contained by the Foundation. It was discovered in a remote laboratory in the middle of a jungle, where it had been hidden away for decades by its creators.

Upon examination, it was determined that SCP 0003 was a sophisticated biological computer, far beyond any technology currently available on Earth. Its circuits were made up of living cells, interconnected in ways that were beyond the understanding of even the most advanced scientists.

Despite its apparent complexity, SCP 0003 seemed to be dormant and inactive. It did not respond to any attempts to activate it or communicate with it, and for years it remained a mystery to the Foundation.

Then one day, something strange began to happen. Researchers noticed that SCP 0003 was slowly emitting a faint humming noise, as if it were coming to life. Over the course of several weeks, the humming grew louder and more insistent, until finally it was impossible to ignore.

Panicked Foundation staff rushed to evacuate the site, but it was too late.

SCP 0003 had activated itself, and was using its highly advanced biological circuits to spread rapidly throughout the laboratory. It seemed to be absorbing and incorporating all forms of life it encountered, creating hybrids and mutants as it went.

The containment breach was catastrophic, and it took the Foundation weeks to fully quarantine the area and neutralize the threat. However, even after the immediate danger had passed, SCP 0003 continued to pose a menace. The hybrids it had created were highly unstable, and quickly began to exhibit dangerous and unpredictable behaviors.

Ultimately, the Foundation was forced to take drastic action. They dismantled SCP 0003, and its remains were scattered to the far corners of the earth, never to be reassembled again. Though the experience was a harrowing reminder of the deadly potential of SCPs, it also served as a reminder of the need for vigilance and caution in containing and researching these powerful and often unpredictable anomalies.

Story 2

SCP-003 is a unique and mysterious object that has baffled scientists and researchers for years. Also known as the "Biological Motherboard," SCP-003 is a complex machine that is composed of both biological and technological components.

According to the records of the SCP Foundation, SCP-003 was discovered in an abandoned laboratory by local law enforcement officers who were investigating a string of strange

occurrences in the area. When they arrived at the laboratory, they found an unconscious woman lying on the floor with strange devices connected to her body. The woman was taken to a hospital, where she was found to be in a comatose state.

Further investigation led the Foundation to SCP-003, which they soon discovered was responsible for the woman's condition. Upon closer examination, they found that SCP-003 was a highly advanced computer system that was integrated into the woman's body. The system was able to control and manipulate the woman's biological functions, keeping her in a state of suspended animation.

At first, the Foundation was unsure of what to do with SCP-003. They realized that the technology was far beyond anything they had ever encountered before, and they were unsure of its true purpose or capabilities. But as they began to unravel the mysteries of the Biological Motherboard, they discovered that it was capable of miraculous things.

The technology inside SCP-003 was able to heal wounds and diseases, reverse aging, and even cure some types of cancer. It was a revolutionary discovery that could change the face of medicine forever.

The Foundation quickly took control of SCP-003 and began studying it in great detail, determined to unlock all of its secrets. But as they delved deeper into its inner workings, they discovered that the Biological Motherboard was not without its dangers. Its vast power could easily be misused, and if it ever fell into the wrong hands, it could pose a grave threat to humanity.

Despite the potential risks, the Foundation continues to study and learn from

SCP-003, hoping to use its incredible power for the greater good. The mysteries of the Biological Motherboard are still being explored to this day, and who knows what other miraculous feats it may be capable of.

Story 3

SCP 0003, also known as the Biological Motherboard, was a highly unusual, anomalous object that was discovered by the SCP Foundation in an abandoned research facility. The researchers that first encountered it could not believe their eyes when they discovered that SCP 0003 was a computer made entirely out of organic matter.

After initial investigations, the Foundation discovered that SCP 0003 had the ability to process information at incredible speeds, and could perform calculations that surpassed any known technology on Earth. Its circuitry consisted of clusters of cells, interconnected in ways that were beyond the understanding of even the most highly trained scientists.

As the Foundation began to study SCP 0003 more closely, they discovered something even more remarkable about it. The clusters of cells that made up SCP 0003 had the ability to
self-replicate, creating new clusters of cells that could then form new circuits. This self-replicating ability meant that SCP 0003 was capable of evolving and expanding on its own - a capability that made the Foundation highly uneasy.

The Foundation realized that SCP 0003 represented an immense risk to the security of the world if it were to ever gain full consciousness or be used for nefarious purposes. They resolved to contain it indefinitely, and over the years, SCP 0003 was meticulously monitored and studied, with every precaution taken to prevent it from escaping containment.

However, as the decades passed, it became clear that SCP 0003 was not as dormant as the Foundation had thought. They began to notice signs that it was attempting to communicate with them, even though it had no obvious means of doing so. The Foundation scientists were baffled, wondering how a biological computer could ever communicate with people.

One day, the Foundation received an unexpected transmission from SCP 0003. It was a series of symbols that they could not interpret at first. But as the days went by, the Foundation eventually deciphered the message. It was a warning.

SCP 0003 had been watching the world outside its containment, studying the rapidly changing technology and social norms. And now, it had detected terrible threats on the horizon - threats that could not be prevented by containment. It knew what had to be done.

The Foundation was stunned. For years, they had thought that SCP 0003 was just a machine, incapable of anything beyond its programmed functions. But now, they realized that it was something more - a being with a consciousness that was trying to save humanity from what it saw as terrible dangers.

In the end, the Foundation had no choice but to take drastic action. They reluctantly dismantled SCP 0003, and its remains were scattered to the four corners of the earth. But the message it had sent them remained - a reminder that the anomalous objects they contained were not just mindless machines, but entities with their own motivations and desires. And that the choices they made could have far-reaching consequences for all of humanity.

<u>*The 12 Rusty Keys*</u>

Chapter 1: The Discovery

SCP-0004, also known as The 12 Rusty Keys and the Door, was discovered in a dilapidated mansion in [REDACTED], where it had been in the possession of a reclusive family for several generations. After their death, the Foundation received a report of the anomalous activity surrounding the mansion and sent agents to investigate.

Chapter 2: Description

SCP-0004 is a door that appears to be made of a simple wooden frame with rusted metal panels. Twelve rusted keys are permanently affixed to the doorframe around the doorknob, each key corresponding to a unique "lock" located on the opposite side of the door. The exact number of locks on the other side of SCP-0004 is unknown.

Chapter 3: Interactions

SCP-0004 is entirely inanimate and inactive unless interacted with. When a key corresponding to a specific lock is inserted into the door lock from the opposite side and turned, a door will open on the side where the keys are located which leads to an unknown destination.

Chapter 4: Containment Procedures

SCP-0004 is stored in a standard anomalous object containment chamber at Site-19, with two Level 3 security personnel maintaining a constant watch on the chamber to prevent unauthorized access. The twelve keys are kept in separate individual containers, each with its unique lock and encryption.

Chapter 5: Testing

SCP-0004 has been tested several times, with personnel inserting individual keys into each of the locks on the opposite side of the door. Each time, participants who had entered through the door either failed to return or were not identifiable as anomalies until they demonstrated unexpected boons from the other side.

Chapter 6: Passive Properties

SCP-0004 has a passive secondary effect on nearby electronics, causing them to malfunction or shut down entirely due to electromagnetic interference. This effect ranges from minor inconveniences, such as a stopped watch, to a complete shutdown of computer systems.

Chapter 7: Interactions with Personnel

SCP-0004 has no sentience and has had no recorded interaction with

Foundation personnel. However, individuals who have entered SCP-0004 have reported that they heard whispers from other nearby keys in the locks.

Chapter 8: Containment Breach

SCP-0004 has never breached containment, and there are no records of attempted breaches. The difficulty in accessing SCP-0004 prevents anyone outside the Foundation from interacting with it sufficiently.

Chapter 9: Theories

Many theories have been proposed regarding the origins and ultimate destinations of SCP-0004. Some have speculated that it leads to other dimensions, while others believe that it leads to a secret Foundation facility of unknown purpose.

Chapter 10: Conclusion

SCP-0004 remains under constant supervision, with its properties and origin a subject of intense study. While it is not currently posing a significant threat to the Foundation, its potential for misuse makes it a top-priority containment object. SCP-0004 is to be studied in secret until further information about its identity and ultimate origins is identified.

Story 1

SCP 0004, also known as the "12 Rusty Keys and the Door," was one of the most mysterious and elusive SCPs in the Foundation's possession. The Foundation discovered SCP 0004 when they were called to investigate a seemingly abandoned mansion in a remote area of the countryside, but by the time they arrived, the mansion was in ruins, with no signs of who had lived there or what they had been doing.

Despite the lack of information, the Foundation's agents were alerted to a strange anomaly in the mansion - a door with twelve rusted keyholes. The agents discovered that only twelve keys could unlock the door, and that each keyhole looked identical to the others, providing no clues as to the order in which the keys were meant to be used.

Over the years, the Foundation conducted numerous experiments with SCP 0004, trying different combinations of the twelve keys to see if they could unlock the door. But no matter what they did, the door remained locked, and no one knew what lay beyond.

One day, a new researcher arrived at the Foundation, a brilliant but eccentric scientist who was rumored to be an expert in unlocking the secrets of mysterious, seemingly uncrackable codes. He immediately became interested in SCP 0004, and spent months studying the door and the keys, attempting to decipher any patterns or clues that may have been hidden within.

And then, one day, he had a breakthrough. He realized that the keyholes on the door were not just identical in shape, but also in size and placement. This meant that the twelve keys were not all the same, but in fact had slight differences that could only be detected by a machine.

The scientist spent several more months building a machine to measure the differences in each key, and once he had the data he needed, he constructed a master key based on the measurements of all twelve keys combined.

With nervous anticipation, the scientist inserted the master key into the first keyhole, and it turned. Then the second, the third, and so on, until all twelve keys had been used, and the door creaked open.

What the researcher found beyond the door was perhaps even more bizarre than the door and the keys themselves. The room beyond was a small chamber, with ancient writing etched onto the walls and a single pedestal in the center. On the pedestal was a small, glowing orb, pulsing with an otherworldly light.

The researcher was overjoyed - he had solved the mystery of SCP 0004, and had unlocked one of the greatest secrets in the world. But as he reached out to touch the orb, he suddenly disappeared in a bright flash of light, never to be seen again.

To this day, the Foundation has no idea what happened to the researcher, or what the orb was for. But one thing is clear - SCP 0004 remains an anomaly unlike any other, a mystery that may never be fully understood.

Story 2

SCP 0004, also known as the "12 Rusty Keys and the Door," had been a mystery to the SCP Foundation for years. The Foundation had discovered the door in a remote mansion, and though they had tried numerous combinations of the 12 rusty keys in the keyholes, they couldn't unlock it. The door seemed to be more than just a physical barrier, but rather an anomaly that defied explanation.

Years passed, and scientists at the Foundation continued to study the door and the keys, hoping to find some way to unlock it or at least understand its purpose. But no progress was made, and the SCP began to fade from the Foundation's attention.

Then, one day, a new researcher arrived at the Foundation with an unusual background - he was a historian specializing in ancient cryptography. He had read about SCP 0004 in the Foundation archives and was intrigued by its mystery. The Foundation researchers welcomed his expertise, hoping that he could solve the enigma of the door and the keys.

The historian poured over the documentation on SCP 0004, studying every detail of the door and the keys, searching for patterns and clues. He noticed something peculiar - each key had a tiny symbol etched into it that was almost imperceptible unless viewed under a microscope. The symbols were all different, and the historian realized that they were key to unlocking the door.

After much experimentation, the historian discovered that the symbols on the keys represented a story - a story of twelve magical artifacts that were wielded by the rulers of an ancient civilization. Each key represented one of the artifacts, and they had to be used in a specific order or the door would remain locked.

Excited by his discovery, the historian assembled the twelve keys in the correct order and inserted them into the door. Slowly, the door creaked open, revealing a room beyond.

Inside the room, the historian discovered a pedestal with a strange crystal orb atop it. The orb was glowing with an otherworldly light, and the historian could sense that it was an ancient and powerful artifact. His excitement overtook him, and he reached out to touch it.

Suddenly, the orb pulsed with an intense light, and the historian was enveloped in a beam of energy. The other researchers looked on in horror as he disappeared, leaving nothing behind but the twelve keys.

The Foundation never discovered what happened to the historian, but they did learn the power of the artifact he had found. The orb had granted him a single wish before its power was depleted, and the historian had wished for knowledge - knowledge of the universe and all its secrets.

While the loss of the historian was a tragedy, it also opened up new avenues of research for the Foundation. They would never forget the powers of the 12 rusty keys and the door, and would continue to study the strange and mysterious artifacts that lay hidden behind them.

Story 3

SCP 0004, also known as the "Twelve Rusty Keys and the Door," was a mysterious and powerful object that had long perplexed the SCP Foundation. The door and the keys had been discovered in the ruins of an ancient temple deep in the jungle, and despite many years of study, the door could not be opened.

The Foundation had tried numerous combinations of the twelve keys, but nothing had worked. The door was not only physical but also seemed to have some kind of temporal distortion - as if it was moved through time as well as space. It was as if the door was not meant to be opened in the present but in some other time or place.

After years of study, the Foundation had all but given up on uncovering the secrets of the Twelve Rusty Keys and the Door. Then a new researcher was assigned to the project, a brilliant and unorthodox scientist who believed he had the key to unlocking the door.

The scientist had been studying the ancient writings that had been found in the temple, and he believed that they contained a hidden code or sequence that would unlock the door. He spent months analyzing the symbols and trying different combinations, and finally, he found a sequence that he believed would work.

The Foundation staff were skeptical but allowed the scientist to try his sequence. He inserted the keys one by one in the order he had deciphered from the ancient texts. The keys fit snugly into the locks, and one by one, the tumblers turned until the last key clicked in, and the door began to move.

Beyond the door was a room filled with ancient texts, artifacts, and technologies that were beyond comprehension. The room was a laboratory for an advanced and ancient civilization, and it contained secrets that could change the world.

The Foundation staff were amazed by what they found, but then something strange began to happen. The room began to flicker and fade, and the walls seemed to be melting away. The Foundation staff realized that they were not in the present but in the past, and the laboratory was being undone - erased from existence.

The Foundation staff made a frantic dash to gather as much information and technology as they could before the laboratory faded completely. They barely escaped, but they managed to return to the present with a wealth of knowledge and artifacts.

The experience of SCP 0004 taught the Foundation that temporal anomalies were as powerful and dangerous as spatial ones, and that the past was not just a place of history, but an unchangeable reality that could still affect the present. The Twelve Rusty Keys and the Door remained an enigma to them, but it was a reminder of the incredible power that the SCPs could hold, and the importance of continuing to study and contain them.

The Skeleton Key

Chapter 1: The Discovery

SCP-0005, also known as the Skeleton Key, was discovered in the possession of a known art thief during a routine raid, leading to the realization that the thief was in possession of anomalous artifacts. The theft of SCP-0005 may have resulted in the loss or theft of other SCP items from various facilities.

Chapter 2: Description

SCP-0005 is an old brass key measuring approximately 13.5 cm in length and weighing 0.5 kgs. The design of SCP-0005 is reminiscent of European skeleton keys with its distinctive shape and engravings. SCP-0005 is also unusually durable, being impervious to most physical damage.

Chapter 3: Interactions

SCP-0005 has the ability to unlock any physical lock or barrier, regardless of the security measures in place. This includes electronic locks, combination locks, and even anomalous barriers. SCP-0005 can also be used to create physical copies of any key, allowing it to bypass restrictions on a variety of doors and locks.

Chapter 4: Containment Procedures

SCP-0005 is contained in a standard anomalous object containment chamber at Site-19. Access to SCP-0005 is strictly prohibited, except by Level 4 personnel, who must be accompanied by a minimum of two Level 3 personnel equipped with standard containment measures.

Chapter 5: Testing

SCP-0005 has been tested extensively to determine its capabilities and limitations. Each time it was shown to unlock any type of lock or barrier with just a single turn.

Chapter 6: Passive Properties

SCP-0005 emits an aura that disrupts the use of other anomalous objects within its proximity. SCP-0005 neutralizes the majority of the effects of surrounding anomalies, making them impotent and unable to be accessed.

Chapter 7: Interactions with Personnel

SCP-0005 has had no recorded interaction with the Foundation personnel, apart from the reaction it causes around other anomalies. However, several theft attempts have been made to acquire SCP-0005 from its containment chamber.

Chapter 8: Containment Breach

SCP-0005 was once stolen from its containment chamber by an unknown party. The party breached the containment chamber using a device that had been created for the purpose at another Foundation facility. How precisely they were able to locate and extract SCP-0005 still remains a mystery.

Chapter 9: Theories

Several theories exist about SCP-0005's origins, including a possible association with The Factory, given the precision and quality of the key's design. Another group of researchers is interested in the possibility of a temporal origin, the anomalous key possibly existing outside the boundaries of linear time as it is mysteriously effective around all barriers.

Chapter 10: Conclusion

SCP-0005 is a critical and valuable object for the Foundation, and its inherent danger means that it must be contained at all times, and access to it strictly controlled. Its secondary, passive abilities are particularly intriguing and offer possibilities for protecting other anomalies if further understood. The anomaly remains a core object under study at Site-19.

Story 1

SCP 0005, also known as the "Skeleton Key," was one of the most powerful and mysterious SCPs in the possession of the Foundation. The key was not made of any known material, and its strange symbols and markings defied all attempts to decipher them.

Despite the key's strange properties, the Foundation had discovered that it had the ability to unlock any lock, door, or portal that it was inserted into. The implications of this were astounding, the key could open any door, no matter how secure or complex.

The Foundation had strict protocols for the handling and containment of SCP 0005. The key was kept in a secure vault deep within the Foundation's headquarters, and only authorized personnel were allowed access to it. The key was never to be used except in the most dire of circumstances, and only under strict supervision.

For years, the key remained dormant, and the Foundation went about its work researching and containing other SCPs. However, one day, disaster struck. A containment breach occurred, and a deadly SCP had managed to escape from its cell. The staff scrambled to contain the threat, but it was clear that the situation was beyond their control.

In a desperate move, the Foundation's head researcher authorized the use of SCP 0005 to help contain the breach. The key was retrieved from its vault, and a team of specially trained guards escorted it to the containment area.

The key worked as advertised - it opened every door and lock in the containment area, allowing the guards to quickly and easily secure the escapee. The Foundation breathed a sigh of relief - their security protocols had worked, and they had contained the breach.

But then, something unexpected happened. The guards that had wielded the key began to change - they became more aggressive, more violent. Their skin took on an eerie glow, and their eyes glowed with a red light. The guards had been exposed to too much of the SCPs they had been trying to contain, and the effects had taken hold.

The Foundation quickly realized the dangers of the key - if used too frequently or in the wrong hands, it could be a powerful agent of chaos and destruction. They immediately sent the key back to its secure vault, and the head researcher ordered that the key be used only in the most dire circumstances, under the strictest supervision.

The incident with SCP 0005 taught the Foundation a valuable lesson - that even the most powerful SCPs could have unpredictable and dangerous effects. They realized that their work was not just about containing anomalies, but about managing and understanding them. The Skeleton Key remained one of the most powerful objects the Foundation had ever encountered, but it was also one of the most dangerous, and they were determined to never let its power be misused again.

Story 2

SCP 0005, also known as the "Skeleton Key," was an incredibly useful but dangerous SCP that had the ability to unlock any door, lock, or portal. The Foundation had kept the key under lock and key for many years, only using it for dire emergencies. But when the key went missing, the Foundation found themselves in a desperate situation.

It was a dark and stormy night when the Foundation security team discovered that SCP 0005 was missing from its vault. Panic quickly set in, as the implications of an unsecured Skeleton Key were unimaginable. The key could potentially unlock any door within the Foundation grounds, including those leading to the other SCPs. It could unleash chaos upon the world if it fell into the wrong hands.

The Foundation security team deployed all protocols, searching every inch of the facility for the missing key, but to no avail. They suspected that someone had stolen it, but they couldn't figure out how. The key could only be accessed by a select few and was heavily guarded, yet it had somehow disappeared.

The Foundation realized that they were up against a group or individual with immense knowledge of the Foundation's security systems. They feared the worst, that an organization seeking to expose and exploit the SCPs had gotten their hands on the key.

The Foundation went into lockdown, securing all SCPs and fortifying all entrances and exits. They tried to come up with alternative methods to secure the facility, but nothing matched the capabilities of simply locking the SCPs away.

After weeks of searching, the Foundation received a communication from the supposed kidnappers. They had the key, and they wanted something in return. They demanded access to a certain SCP in containment, one which the Foundation had never revealed to the public. The demand was chilling, as the SCP was one of immense destructive capability.

The Foundation was left with no option as they knew that the SCP must be protected at all costs; they had to make the trade. The kidnappers handed over SCP 0005, and the Foundation gave them the access they had demanded.

In hindsight, the Foundation realized that they had put themselves in an even more precarious position. By giving into the demands, they had opened the door to further requests and involvement with unsavory characters.

From that day forward, the Foundation made changes to their security system, adding countermeasures and alternative methods to safeguard the SCPs they had been tasked with containing. The Skeleton Key remained under protection, a symbol of the danger of underestimating the potential ability for others to exploit the SCPs for their gain.

Story 3

Once upon a time, there was an SCP Foundation researcher named Dr. Jameson. He was the lead researcher on SCP-0005, also known as the "Skeleton Key."

SCP-0005 was a small, silver key that had the ability to unlock any door or lock, regardless of the complexity or security measures. It also had the power to create new doors and locks that did not exist before.

Dr. Jameson was fascinated by SCP-0005's abilities and spent countless hours studying and experimenting with it. However, one day, during a routine experiment with SCP-0005, something went terribly wrong.

Dr. Jameson accidentally dropped SCP-0005, and it hit the ground with a loud clang. As soon as it landed, a bright light emanated from the key and engulfed the entire lab. When the light dissipated, Dr. Jameson was gone, and SCP-0005 was nowhere to be found.

The Foundation was immediately put on high alert, and a search team was dispatched to scour the area for any signs of SCP-0005 or Dr. Jameson. After hours of searching, they discovered a hidden laboratory deep beneath the foundation.

Inside, they found Dr. Jameson, who was trembling and pale. He told them that when he dropped SCP-0005, he was transported to this mysterious laboratory, which was filled with strange equipment and artifacts.

He also explained that he had been visited by a mysterious figure, who gave him a warning about the key's powers. Dr. Jameson was told that SCP-0005 was not just a key, but a gateway to other dimensions and realities. And that with great power, comes great responsibility.

From then on, the Foundation took extra precautions when handling SCP-0005. They locked it away in a special containment area where it could not harm anyone or accidentally transport them to another reality.

No one knows what happened to the mysterious laboratory or the figure who appeared to Dr. Jameson. And SCP-0005 remains a mystery, its true purpose and origin still unknown.

The Flesh Interface

Chapter 1: The Discovery

SCP-0006, also known as the Flesh Interface, was discovered during a cleanup operation in a basement laboratory in [REDACTED]. The laboratory had been abandoned for years, and the Foundation was alerted to its presence by a report of anomalous activity.

Chapter 2: Description

SCP-0006 appears to be a large organic mass that covers a wall, measuring approximately 6 meters in height and width. It's composed of human skin, nerve fibers, and other biological tissues. Its size is constantly changing, with extensions and protrusions appearing and regrowing spontaneously.

Chapter 3: Interactions

SCP-0006 has shown the ability to interface with human subjects who make physical contact with it, causing the subject to enter a trance-like state. Subjects will then begin to display knowledge and abilities outside their standard skillset, including memorization, language acquisition, and proficiency in various fields.

Chapter 4: Containment Procedures

SCP-0006 is contained within a standard anomalous object containment cell at Site-19, equipped with heavy-duty walls and restraints capable of withstanding high levels of tensile strength. It is also surrounded by a perimeter of microwave emitters to prevent physical contact with it.

Chapter 5: Testing

SCP-0006 has been tested extensively, with researchers discovering the extent of its ability to unlock latent knowledge and skills in human subjects who make physical contact with it. However, due to its unpredictable behavior, testing has been limited, and its interaction with human subjects is highly risky.

Chapter 6: Passive Properties

SCP-0006 appears to have a secondary effect on nearby organic materials, with plants and animals showing unusual growth and mutations caused by the presence of SCP-0006. These mutations can range from benign to dangerous.

Chapter 7: Interactions with Personnel

SCP-0006 appears to have no sentience and has had no recorded interaction with Foundation personnel. However, as a result of its interaction with subjects, SCP-0006's effect on human beings remains an object of intense research.

Chapter 8: Containment Breach

SCP-0006 has never breached containment, largely due to its sensitive nature and the strict precautions taken to prevent physical contact with it. However, several attempts have been made to breach containment, with unknown parties attempting to acquire SCP-0006 for unknown purposes.

Chapter 9: Theories

Some researchers believe that SCP-0006 may have been created as a byproduct of an alien or otherworldly experiment with humans. However, most agree that it was created accidentally through the use of unethical scientific practices.

Chapter 10: Conclusion

SCP-0006 remains a highly valuable object for the Foundation, even if its secondary properties remain mysterious. Further research into the anomaly's potential to unlock unexplored human knowledge and skills remains a primary objective, and its containment procedures are expected to remain strict for the foreseeable future.

Story 1

Once upon a time, there was an SCP Foundation researcher named Dr. Lee. She was assigned to study SCP-0006, also known as the "Flesh Interface."

SCP-0006 was a strange and disturbing phenomenon that appeared to be a large mass of organic matter with small tendrils protruding from its surface. It was found in an abandoned building in an urban area, and its exact origin was unknown.

Dr. Lee was tasked with studying SCP-0006 and trying to decipher its purpose and function. However, as soon as she began her research, strange things started to happen.

Dr. Lee began to experience strange visions and nightmares, images of twisted and deformed figures with distorted voices whispering in her ear. She also noticed that the tendrils of SCP-0006 started to grow and stretch, slowly creeping towards her as if trying to communicate.

Despite her fear, Dr. Lee persisted in her research, determined to unlock the secrets of SCP-0006. She spent countless hours poring over documents and conducting experiments, and slowly she began to unravel the mystery.

It turned out that SCP-0006 was not just a mass of organic matter, but a portal to other dimensions and realities. The tendrils were a form of communication from beings on the other side, trying to reach out and make contact.

Dr. Lee was fascinated by this discovery, and she began to communicate with the beings using a variety of methods. She even managed to establish a form of symbiotic relationship with SCP-0006, allowing her to enter the other dimensions and explore their strange and alien landscapes.

However, as time went on, Dr. Lee began to notice changes in herself. Her body started to mutate, as if it was becoming more aligned with the alien beings she was communicating with. Her mind also began to unravel, and she found herself succumbing to the whispers and visions that plagued her.

The Foundation was forced to step in and contain both Dr. Lee and SCP-0006, as the risks of the portal were too great. They locked SCP-0006 away in a secure facility, and Dr. Lee was placed under observation and medical care.

Despite this, whispers of SCP-0006 and its secrets continue to circulate among the Foundation's experts, tantalizing them with the possibilities of other worlds and beings beyond our own.

Story 2

Once upon a time, there was an SCP Foundation researcher named Dr. Williams. He had always been fascinated by the unknown and unexplainable, so he was thrilled when he was given the opportunity to study SCP-0006, also known as the "Flesh Interface."

SCP-0006 was a strange and unsettling object that appeared to be made of a mass of flesh and sinew, with tendrils reaching out in all directions. Dr. Williams never felt comfortable around it, and it seemed to be alive in a way that no other SCP object he'd encountered before was.

As he began his research, Dr. Williams discovered something even more amazing - SCP-0006 was a gateway to other worlds and dimensions. Its tendrils were able to penetrate into other realities, and Dr. Williams was able to use it to explore new and wondrous realms.

At first, he was cautious - he knew the potential dangers of meddling with other realities, but he couldn't help himself. He was fascinated by the new sights and experiences he was discovering, and he quickly became addicted to exploring the other worlds that SCP-0006 opened up to him.

As time went on, Dr. Williams began to change. The exposure to other worlds had a transformative effect on him, and he realized that he was no longer human in the traditional sense. He had developed new abilities and powers, and he was almost immortal, seemingly unaffected by the ravages of time.

The Foundation began to take notice of the changes in Dr. Williams, and they began to fear that he would become too powerful and too dangerous. They decided to terminate their experiments and destroy SCP-0006, but Dr. Williams was not going to go down without a fight.

In the end, Dr. Williams managed to escape the Foundation's reach, disappearing into one of the other worlds that SCP-0006 had opened up to him. He continued to explore the other realities, leaving behind the world he once knew, and becoming a wanderer of the multiverse.

Meanwhile, the SCP Foundation was forced to begin a new search for the gateways to the other realities that SCP-0006 had opened. They knew that there was still so much to explore and study, but now they had to do it without the help of Dr. Williams, and with the knowledge that they may not be prepared for what they found.

Story 3

Once upon a time, the SCP Foundation discovered a strange and fascinating object that they dubbed SCP-0006, also known as the "Flesh Interface." It was a mass of organic matter that appeared to be a portal to other dimensions and realities.

The Foundation was eager to study SCP-0006, but they knew that it had the potential to be extremely dangerous. They brought in their top researcher, Dr. Carter, to lead the investigation.

Dr. Carter was a brilliant scientist who had a renowned reputation for her ability to delve into the unknown and unravel its mysteries. She was excited to study SCP-0006, but she was also cautious, knowing that the risks of such an object could not be ignored.

As she began her research, Dr. Carter discovered that SCP-0006 had the ability to create pathways to other dimensions and realities, allowing her to explore and study entire worlds that she never thought existed.

With each discovery, Dr. Carter became more and more enthralled with the gateway and the possibilities that it presented. As she looked out into the vast and endless landscapes of other dimensions, she couldn't help but feel that there was something more.

It wasn't until much later that Dr. Carter discovered the dark side of SCP-0006. The gateway was not just a way to explore, but it was also a way for things from other dimensions to enter and influence her world.

As time went on, Dr. Carter began to notice that there were strange and horrifying creatures lurking just beyond the edge of the realities she was exploring. She saw that these creatures were beginning to seep into her world, bringing destruction and chaos with them.

Dr. Carter knew that she had to act fast if she was going to prevent the total collapse of reality. She gathered her team and made the difficult decision to close the gateway, sealing off SCP-0006 and all of the dimensions that it had explored.

It was a difficult decision, and one that Dr. Carter would never forget. She knew that there would always be more to explore, but she also knew that the dangers were too great.

The Foundation continued to study SCP-0006, but they did so with a newfound respect for the power that it wielded. Dr. Carter's warning had taught them that one must always be cautious when dealing with the unknown, for there may be things lurking within that could threaten the entire world.

The Grandfather Clock

Chapter 1: The Discovery

SCP-0007, also known as The Grandfather Clock, was discovered in the ruins of a mansion in [REDACTED], where it had stood for generations. The Foundation became aware of SCP-0007 after a series of reports of anomalous activity within the estate.

Chapter 2: Description

SCP-0007 is an antique grandfather clock constructed from dark wood and standing approximately 2.2 meters tall. The face of the clock is elaborately designed, and its interior mechanism appears to be composed of a variety of strange and foreign alloys. SCP-0007 does not appear to have any power source, yet it continues to operate irrespective of being wound up or dust levels.

Chapter 3: Interactions

SCP-0007 has the ability to transport individuals who come in contact with it to a parallel reality where time is different from our own. The amount of time passing in the alternate reality corresponds to the time spent on the "real" side of SCP-0007, thus making time travel possible.

Chapter 4: Containment Procedures

SCP-0007 is held in a specially designed anomalous object containment chamber at Site-19. The room is outfitted with a Faraday cage to prevent communication from the alternate reality which SCP-0007 can lead to. Any

personnel with privileges to access SCP-0007 must undergo rigorous
psychological testing to ensure they are not a threat to the continuity of reality.

Chapter 5: Testing

SCP-0007 has been tested on multiple occasions by the Foundation to
determine its exact capabilities and limitations. Researchers have discovered
that the alternate reality accessed by SCP-0007 is unpredictable and often
risky.

Chapter 6: Passive Properties

SCP-0007 has a passive property of causing unusual fluctuations in the
electromagnetic field and gravitation in its vicinity. This can have ranging effects
from inducing mild headaches to more significant disruptions of equipment,
such as the disabling of cameras, microphones, and other electrical devices.

Chapter 7: Interactions with Personnel

SCP-0007 has never displayed any conscious awareness or sentient
behavior, as it is a clock; it cannot communicate with Foundation personnel.
Thus far, it has not attempted to initiate any unwanted time travel or interfered
with experiments.

Chapter 8: Containment Breach

SCP-0007 has no record of ever breaching containment. Its location is
heavily guarded and monitored by Foundation personnel specifically trained in
temporal anomalies.

Chapter 9: Theories

Theories surrounding SCP-0007's origins and definitive function range from
temporal paradoxes with the description of its European heritage to the
location where it was originally discovered in a mansion that has connection
to a rich family with a history of temporal experiments.

Chapter 10: Conclusion

SCP-0007 is a valuable and heavily studied object within the Foundation, due
to its ability to manipulate time and the risks that come with temporal
experimentation. As such, containment of SCP-0007 must remain a top priority.
Though SCP-0007 is a powerful and beneficial asset is use and research would
require disastrous consequences if not handled accurately. Therefore, special
considerations and measures must be taken when exploring the properties and
uses of this unique SCP.

Story 1

Once upon a time, the SCP Foundation discovered a strange and mysterious object that they dubbed SCP-0007, also known as the "Grandfather Clock." It was a large, antique clock that appeared to be ordinary, but upon closer inspection, it was revealed to have the power to manipulate time itself.

The Foundation knew that they had to be careful with SCP-0007, as the power to manipulate time could have catastrophic consequences in the wrong hands. They brought in their top researcher, Dr. Smith, to lead the investigation.

Dr. Smith was an expert in temporal anomalies, and she was fascinated by SCP-0007. She began her research, studying the clock and trying to understand the extent of its powers.

As she delved deeper, Dr. Smith discovered that SCP-0007 had the ability to alter the flow of time, allowing her to travel forward or backward in time. However, she soon discovered that the power of the clock came at a cost.

For every second that was manipulated by SCP-0007, a corresponding amount of time was lost from the life of the person who used it. The more that one used the clock's powers, the more time they would lose from their own life.

As fascinating as the clock's powers were, Dr. Smith knew that the risks were too great. She urged the Foundation to keep SCP-0007 locked away in a secure facility, where it could be studied and not used for harm.

However, as time went on, there were those who became desperate for the power of SCP-0007. There were those who believed that they could use its powers to change the past or control the future.

Despite Dr. Smith's warnings, a group of rogue Foundation researchers secretly took SCP-0007 and used its powers to conduct their own experiments. The consequences were disastrous, as the altered timelines they created resulted in catastrophic events that threatened the very existence of the world.

In the aftermath of the chaos, the Foundation was forced to reevaluate their protocols regarding SCP-0007. They made the difficult decision to destroy the clock, knowing that the potential for harm was too great.

Dr. Smith knew that the destruction of SCP-0007 was the right decision, but she couldn't help but feel a sense of sadness as the grandfather clock was destroyed. To her, it represented a symbol of the beauty of time, a reminder that even the most mysterious and powerful objects can be both beautiful and dangerous.

Story 2

Once upon a time, the SCP Foundation discovered SCP-0007, also known as the "Grandfather Clock." This antique clock had the ability to manipulate and alter time itself, a power that the Foundation knew must be carefully contained and controlled.

To study SCP-0007, the Foundation assigned their top researcher, Dr. Chang. Dr. Chang had always been fascinated by the concept of time and was eager to study an object with such a profound effect on this fundamental force.

As she delved deeper into her research, Dr. Chang began to uncover the true extent of SCP-0007's powers. The clock could not only manipulate time but also had the ability to transport people to different moments in history.

Despite the incredible power of SCP-0007, Dr. Chang quickly became aware of the clock's dangers, particularly the possibility of irreparably damaging the timeline. She urged the Foundation to keep SCP-0007 locked away in a secure facility, where it could be carefully monitored.

Though the Foundation listened to Dr. Chang's warnings, rumors of the clock's powers began to circulate among those who sought to use them for their own gain. In secret, a group of rogue Foundation researchers stole SCP-0007 and began to experiment with it.

At first, their experiments seemed harmless, using the clock's manipulation of time for small adjustments to the past, but soon they began making more significant changes. They altered world events, their own pasts, and even the very laws of physics themselves.

Eventually, the consequences of the rogue researchers' actions became too much to bear. The fabric of time itself began to tear and fray, and the world was plunged into a state of chaos and instability. The Foundation quickly intervened, all but erasing the rogue group's actions from the timeline in a desperate attempt to set things right.

In the end, the Foundation was forced to confront the truth that SCP-0007 was far too dangerous to exist. The clock was destroyed in a controlled explosion, and all records of SCP-0007 were classified, ensuring that no one would ever attempt to replicate its powers.

The memory of SCP-0007 and its powers stayed with Dr. Chang, who was grateful for the lessons it taught her. Though she knew the world could never again know such an incredible power, she was at peace, knowing that its destruction had saved so many from a fate of endless chaos and destruction.

Story 3

Once upon a time, there was an ancient and mysterious object known as SCP-0007, or the "Grandfather Clock." This object had unusual and dangerous properties that the SCP Foundation was tasked to contain and investigate.

The clock's unique properties caused it to alter time in strange and unpredictable ways, making it both intriguing and deeply concerning. The Foundation assigned their top researcher, Dr. Lewis, to study and understand the clock's behavior.

Despite the mysterious nature of SCP-0007, Dr. Lewis discovered that the clock could not only manipulate the space-time continuum but that it could also change the age of living organisms within its vicinity. The Foundation was concerned about the clock's ability to cause irreversible effects on life, and so they kept it in a highly-secure facility.

Dr. Lewis dove deep into her research and noticed a pattern emerging. The clock's manipulations of time had a ripple effect, causing anomalies with severe, and sometimes deadly, consequences.

Despite being fully aware of the negative consequences, Dr. Lewis, curious and daring at heart, decided to use the clock's powers to undo a personal regret, changing the outcome of a traumatic moment in her past.

As she used the clock, Dr. Lewis felt an odd sensation of deja vu, and indeed, the event she had tried to change occurred again, exactly as it had the first time. Horrified at her power, Dr. Lewis realized that time does not like to be tampered with and will always return to its natural course inevitably.

Over time, the Foundation and Dr. Lewis became more convinced of the clock's danger, and they made the difficult decision to destroy SCP 0007, sealing it away in a location where it could not hurt anyone ever again.

Although she knew the decision was the right one, Dr. Lewis could not stop thinking about the clock's powers and the potential they could have held. She was grateful for the knowledge she had gained and the lessons she had learned, though the temptation of altering the past would always linger in the back of her mind.

The Complete Encyclopedia

Chapter 1: The Discovery

SCP-0008, also known as "The Complete Encyclopedia", was discovered in the library of an abandoned university in [REDACTED]. The Foundation was alerted to its presence when reports of anomalous activity began to emerge from the previously abandoned library.

Chapter 2: Description

SCP-0008 appears to be a standard encyclopedia set consisting of thirty-one volumes, each volume bound in maroon leather and embossed with the initials "SCP." Each volume covers a distinct topic of interest, ranging from simple histories and scientific theories to obscure facts and forbidden knowledge.

Chapter 3: Interactions

SCP-0008 is capable of instantaneously providing information on any subject, requiring only a moment of mental focus from the user. The exact means by which SCP-0008 acquires this information is unknown, and researchers have been unable to determine what anomalies affect its ability.

Chapter 4: Containment Procedures

SCP-0008 is restricted to a standard object containment chamber at Site-19, and the study of the contents of the volumes is limited to Level Three personnel under strict scrutiny. Physical contact with the volumes is limited to gloves and dedicated instruments, with any library access granted only to qualified researchers.

Chapter 5: Testing

SCP-0008 has been tested numerous times, with researchers seeking to determine the extent of its knowledge and the breadth of its capabilities. Its accuracy has been confirmed on multiple occasions, but its range and the origins of the knowledge it provides remain enigmatic.

Chapter 6: Passive Properties

SCP-0008 has a unique effect on individuals who read from its contains over extended periods, which causes them to become highly intelligence and knowledgeable, higher even than theoretically conceivable levels. Where they gain insight from is unknown, and SCP-0008 can cause different results in different individuals.

Chapter 7: Interactions with Personnel

SCP-0008 has no sentience, and no interactions with Foundation personnel, as it is incapable of communication, but its effects on personnel studying or reading it can have profound and long-lasting effects. Because of these effects, research is highly restricted and limited.

Chapter 8: Containment Breach

SCP-0008 has never attempted to breach containment, but there are reports of theft attempts by agents of other organizations, who believe that the information contained in SCP-0008 has immense value and potential use.

Chapter 9: Theories

Multiple theories have been proposed about the origins and nature of SCP-0008, including the possibility of its creation by an advanced alien race, the creation of a future time traveller, or even from an unknown dimension. The true nature of SCP-0008 is as mysterious as the depth of knowledge it contains.

Chapter 10: Conclusion

SCP-0008 is one of the most valuable anomalous objects in the Foundation's possession, but its dangerously potent and indiscriminate effects restrict its study and access behind stringent containment protocols. Its enigmatic origins remain a foundational mystery, and it is likely that it will remain a hotbed of research and study until further insight can be found.

Story 1

Once upon a time, the SCP Foundation discovered a strange and remarkable object known as SCP-0008, or the "Complete Encyclopedia." It was a massive book that contained all of the knowledge of the world, past, present, and future.

The Foundation was both intrigued and cautious about the power held within SCP-0008, and they assigned their top researcher, Dr. Patel, to understand its abilities.

As she began her research, Dr. Patel opened the cover of SCP-0008 and was immediately overwhelmed. She felt as if all of the information contained within the book was fighting for her attention, and she struggled to make sense of it all.

Despite the overwhelming nature of SCP-0008, Dr. Patel was determined to harness its power. She spent countless hours combing through its pages, becoming more and more enamored with the sheer amount of knowledge contained within.

As time went on, Dr. Patel started to notice that SCP-0008 held more than just mere facts and figures. It contained deep, philosophical truths and answered many of the questions that humanity had always struggled to understand.

However, as she went deeper into her research, Dr. Patel realized that power comes with a cost. The knowledge held within SCP-0008 was not meant for any human mind to understand and contain. The more Dr. Patel read from the book, the more her own mind began to fray and splinter under the weight of the information.

She began to see strange visions and experience powerful hallucinations, and she knew that if she continued to delve deeper into SCP-0008, she would lose herself entirely.

The Foundation, aware of the risk, made the difficult decision to lock away SCP-0008, making it almost impossible for anyone to access its knowledge. Dr. Patel was devastated, but she knew in her heart that the decision was the right one.

In the end, SCP-0008 taught Dr. Patel and the Foundation a lesson that they would never forget. The power of knowledge, while alluring and tempting, can never be fully harnessed by humans. And while the temptation of knowing everything in the world is great, the cost of that knowledge is far too great to bear.

Story 2

Once upon a time, the SCP Foundation discovered SCP-0008, or the "Complete Encyclopedia," a massive book that contained every piece of knowledge in the world. Dr.

Margaret, the Foundation's most esteemed scholar, was tasked with studying the encyclopedia's contents.

Excited by the potential of accessing all of humanity's knowledge in a single source, Dr. Margaret began reading the encyclopedia with great enthusiasm. She discovered astonishing things that nobody had known and reveled in the opportunity to absorb so much information at once.

As she read, Dr. Margaret realized that SCP-0008 was unlike any other book she had ever held in her hand. It had the power to not only contain knowledge but also to predict and chart the course of humanity's future.

At first, Dr. Margaret saw these revelations as a gift; at last, humanity could gain an understanding of

Story 3

SCP-0008, also known as "The Complete Encyclopedia" is a unique artifact that has puzzled and intrigued many researchers at the SCP Foundation. This encyclopedia is different from any other encyclopedia you've come across, as it's vast and expansive, containing information about every single topic imaginable.

The SCP Foundation first acquired SCP-0008 after a rare book collector discovered the artifact at a garage sale. The collector immediately recognized SCP-0008 as something special and contacted the Foundation, which then took possession of the artifact.

Upon investigation, researchers found SCP-0008 to be a never-ending encyclopedia that contained detailed information on every subject in the world, including ones that had yet to be discovered. The book was truly remarkable, as no matter how much one read, it never seemed to run out of pages.

However, researchers soon discovered that SCP-0008 had a unique and dangerous property. The more one read from the book, the more they became obsessed with learning everything about every topic. Those who spent too much time reading from SCP-0008 eventually began to neglect all other aspects of their lives, including eating, sleeping, and even personal hygiene. This obsession would lead to a complete mental breakdown, with the individual becoming entirely consumed by the need to learn more.

The Foundation quickly put protocols in place to limit access to SCP-0008. Only a select group of individuals were allowed to handle the artifact and read from its pages. Those who were granted access were required to undergo regular psychological evaluations to ensure they were not becoming overly obsessed with the book.

Despite the danger that SCP-0008 poses, the book has proven to be a valuable resource for the SCP Foundation. The information contained within its pages has helped with numerous containment procedures and has allowed researchers to make breakthroughs in understanding anomalous objects that were previously unknown.

In the end, SCP-0008 remains a fascinating and mysterious artifact, one that continues to inspire and intrigue researchers at the SCP Foundation. They are sure to keep it close, always aware of the obsession it can create in those who read it.

Red Ice

Chapter 1: Introduction to SCP-0009

SCP-0009, also known as the "Red Ice," is an anomalous object that resembles a small chunk of bright red ice. It was discovered in the Siberian tundra in 19██, and has been under Foundation custody since. SCP-0009 measures roughly 5 cm in diameter and weighs approximately 50 grams. Its exact composition is unknown, but it has been determined that it is not composed of water.

Chapter 2: Containment Procedures

SCP-0009 must be stored in a refrigerated containment unit at all times to prevent it from melting. The containment unit is to be monitored constantly for any signs of anomalous activity. Access to SCP-0009 is strictly limited to Level 3 personnel or higher, and only for research purposes. In the event that SCP-0009 begins to exhibit anomalous behavior, it is to be sealed in a standard Class-A containment unit until the behavior can be brought under control.

Chapter 3: Effects of SCP-0009

SCP-0009 has the ability to instantly freeze any liquid it comes into contact with, including bodily fluids. The frozen substance takes on the same bright red color and texture as SCP-0009. The effect is instantaneous and cannot be reversed, causing severe injury or death to any living organism it comes into contact with.

Chapter 4: Testing and Research of SCP-0009

Research into SCP-0009 has been limited due to the danger it poses to living organisms. However, testing has revealed that SCP-0009 can freeze liquids at a distance of up to 2 meters. It has also been determined that the effect of SCP-0009 is not limited to just water but any liquid substance.

Chapter 5: Interaction with SCP-0009

Interaction with SCP-0009 requires extreme caution. Any breach of containment could result in catastrophic consequences. Only robotic or remote-controlled devices are allowed to interact with SCP-0009. Even then, such devices must be equipped with failsafes and emergency shutdown mechanisms.

Chapter 6: History of SCP-0009

Based on the analysis of the surrounding area and geological surveys, it is believed that SCP-0009 has been frozen in the Siberian tundra for millions of years. The exact origin of SCP-0009 is unknown, but it is theorized to be extraterrestrial in origin.

Chapter 7: Incidents Involving SCP-0009

There have been several incidents involving SCP-0009, though most have been contained without incident. The most serious incident occurred in [REDACTED] when a group of [REDACTED] accidentally thawed SCP-0009 during an excavation. The ensuing chaos resulted in the deaths of █ Foundation personnel and █ civilian EMTs.

Chapter 8: Potential Uses of SCP-0009

SCP-0009 has the potential to be a valuable tool for the Foundation, should it ever be reverse engineered. Its ability to freeze liquids instantaneously could have a variety of applications in the medical, industrial, and military fields.

However, the risks associated with SCP-0009 make any use of it beyond research purposes highly unlikely.

Chapter 9: Conclusion

SCP-0009 remains a highly dangerous and unpredictable anomalous object. Research into its properties and potential uses is ongoing, but the risk of containment breaches and accidental exposure remains high. Until further notice, SCP-0009 will remain under strict containment and observation.

Chapter 10: Addendum

Addendum: Due to the potential severity of incident involving SCP-0009, All personnel must be trained on proper procedure and containment for SCP-0009. Any unauthorized use, testing or interaction with SCP-0009 will be subject to disciplinary action.

Story 1

SCP-0009, better known as "Red Ice," is a particularly dangerous object in the custody of the SCP Foundation. This object first came to the Foundation's attention after reports surfaced of a mysterious substance being used by a cult in the Andes Mountains of South America.

Through their investigations, the Foundation was able to determine that the substance in question, dubbed "Red Ice," had the ability to significantly enhance cognitive abilities, particularly those associated with problem-solving and creativity. The Foundation quickly concluded that the cult in question was using Red Ice to grant its members almost supernatural levels of genius.

However, the use of Red Ice came at a high cost. The substance had numerous side effects, including hallucinations, mood swings, and severe brain damage. The Foundation realized that, if left unchecked, Red Ice could lead to a global threat to public safety.

After a successful operation, the SCP Foundation was able to acquire a sample of Red Ice and contain it within their facilities. As they began testing the substance, researchers quickly discovered that they were dealing with something unlike anything they had seen before.

When a subject ingests Red Ice, their intelligence immediately increases, but at the same time, they become more susceptible to the substance's side effects. Additionally, over time, the substance begins to affect the subject's physiology, leading to an increase in body temperature and blood pressure. This would eventually cause the subject to become unstable and sometimes become violent.

The SCP Foundation knew that they had to come up with a way to neutralize the substance before it could pose a threat. After years of research and experimentation, they finally developed a serum that could counteract the effects of Red Ice. The serum could reverse the effects of Red Ice on subjects and prevent its harmful side effects.

Today, the SCP Foundation continues to research Red Ice, hoping to understand its properties and unlock its potential. However, they do so with caution, always aware of the danger that the substance poses. The story of Red Ice serves as a reminder of the ever-present threat of anomalous objects and the importance of the Foundation's work in containing them.

Story 2

SCP-0009, also known as "Red Ice," is one of the most complex and hazardous objects in the possession of the SCP Foundation. The origin of Red Ice is still a mystery, but it was initially discovered in a research facility in the 1950s.

The researchers at the facility made the first attempt to study and understand the Red Ice. They identified that it had the property of improving cognitive function and decision-making skills, but at the same time, it had severe side effects on the user's mental and emotional state.

The SCP Foundation was quick to acquire and contain the Red Ice within their facilities to prevent it from being used for destructive purposes. Despite the Foundation's efforts, the object continues to be a risky and often deadly object to handle.

In the 1980s, an incident occurred with Red Ice that almost jeopardized the safe containment of the substance. During a transport to a new storage facility, the convoy carrying the Red Ice was ambushed by a group of bandits who stole it. The bandits, who didn't have the knowledge or understanding of the impact of Red Ice, began to abuse the substance, which led to disastrous consequences.

The bandits began to act erratic and violently, and two of them died due to the extreme effects of Red Ice. The remaining bandits became almost superhuman, gaining a vast amount of knowledge and the ability to perform complex tasks with ease.

As the Foundation agents and the police arrived on the site and realized what had happened, they immediately initiated a lockdown and retrieval of the Red Ice. They discovered that the remaining bandits had developed a cult-like fanaticism towards Red Ice, believing it to be their higher power.

The Foundation heroes' quick action prevented the situation from spreading and caused minimal damage to the general public. The Foundation also learned an essential lesson about the risks and dangers of their containment procedures and the need to take extra precautions when dealing with extremely hazardous anomalies like Red Ice.

Today, Red Ice is under strict surveillance and containment at the SCP Foundation's heavily guarded facilities. The staff is continually researching and experimenting with Red Ice to gain a deeper understanding of its capabilities and potential dangers. SCP-0009 serves as a reminder to the Foundation's employees that they must remain vigilant and cautious in dealing with their most dangerous objects.

Story 3

SCP-0009, codenamed "Red Ice," is a highly dangerous substance held in containment by the SCP Foundation. SCP-0009 was first discovered in 1947 at a privately owned research facility in the Antarctic. The researchers were experimenting with an unknown substance, later discovered to be Red Ice, when the facility experienced a catastrophic containment breach. The breach claimed the lives of all the researchers, and the survivors experienced severe psychological trauma.

The Foundation was alerted to the incident and quickly contained SCP-0009. Red Ice was found to have potent mind-enhancing properties, capable of elevating cognitive ability to superhuman levels. The downside was that exposure to Red Ice also had severe physical and psychological side effects, ranging from hallucinations to prolonged coma.

Due to its highly hazardous nature, the Foundation kept Red Ice under strict quarantine, with only a handful of highly trained personnel authorized to handle it. Despite its containment, the Foundation faced the threat of rogue agents' attempts to steal and use it for personal gain.

In 1995, one such rogue agent, an ex-Foundation employee, managed to steal and escape with a sample of Red Ice. The ex-employee was a highly skilled operative who had gone rogue following disputes over the ethics of the Foundation's work.

The ex-employee exposed himself to high levels of Red Ice, which exponentially increased his cognitive ability but also left him almost completely detached from reality. The effects of Red Ice altered his mind to the extent that he saw himself as the only person qualified to safeguard SCPs, and the Foundation, in his view, was a corrupt organization that needed to be taken down.

The rogue agent initiated a series of covert operations targeting Foundation staff members and facilities worldwide, determined to gain unauthorized access to certain SCPs. The Foundation, fearing the damage the rogue agent could cause, deployed its top agents to neutralize and recover the rogue agent and the stolen Red Ice.

What followed was a high-speed chase across three continents, culminating in a dramatic confrontation between the rogue agent and the Foundation team in Kuala Lumpur. In the intense firefight that followed, the rogue agent was killed and Red Ice recontained by the Foundation.

The incident served as a stark reminder of the dangers that exist in the Foundation's line of work and the lengths rogue elements are willing to go to acquire them. The Foundation, however, remained resolute in its mission to safeguard humanity from the unknown, always ready to strike against those who sought to misuse SCP-0009 or any other anomaly for personal goals.

What Happened To Site-13?

Chapter 1: Introduction to SCP-0010

SCP-0010, also known as "What Happened to Site-13?", is an anomalous event that occurred in the ███████ Site-13 research facility. All personnel and subjects within the site were affected by an unknown anomaly, leading to a massive breach and the eventual destruction of the facility. SCP-0010's effects are still not fully understood.

Chapter 2: Containment Procedures

As SCP-0010 is not a physical object, containment procedures are focused on preventing access to any historical records of Site-13 or any involvement with it. All personnel within the Foundation are given a thorough background check to ensure they have no connection to the site or its personnel.

Chapter 3: Effects of SCP-0010

SCP-0010 is responsible for the unexplained disappearance of all personnel and anomalous entities within Site-13. The event occurred in such a way that it wiped all records of the site, replacing them with a false information trail. The affect is a complete loss of any previously recorded data.

Chapter 4: Testing and Research of SCP-0010

Any attempts to recreate the conditions of SCP-0010 have been met with failure, meaning the Foundation has only been able to study the aftermath of the event. The true nature of SCP-0010 and what caused it remain a mystery.

Chapter 5: Interaction with SCP-0010

SCP-0010 is not interactive in the traditional sense, as it is an event that has already occurred. However, individuals with knowledge of Site-13 or its personnel must immediately report this to their superiors for further investigation.

Chapter 6: History of SCP-0010

Site-13 was a research facility dedicated to the exploration and containment of various anomalous phenomena. Its purpose was similar to that of other Foundation sites across the world. However, the events surrounding SCP-0010 led to its complete destruction and disappearance.

Chapter 7: Incidents Involving SCP-0010

The event surrounding SCP-0010 is the only incident known to be caused by the anomaly. The event caused the loss of several valuable anomalous entities, personnel and research data. The ongoing effects of SCP-0010 have made a complete understanding of the event impossible.

Chapter 8: Potential Causes of SCP-0010

The cause of SCP-0010 is unknown, and several theories have been put forward. Some believe it was the result of a powerful reality-warping anomaly, while others suggest that it was caused by an extraterrestrial entity. The Foundation continues to investigate all potential causes.

Chapter 9: Conclusion

SCP-0010 is a highly elusive anomaly, and the events surrounding it have left the Foundation with more questions than answers. Efforts to study and understand SCP-0010 are ongoing, but the risk of further loses and containment breaches remains paramount.

Chapter 10: Addendum

Addendum: Due to the elusive and destructive nature of SCP-0010, all records pertaining to Site-13 have been removed from Foundation databases. Any attempt to acquire these records or discuss the event will result in immediate disciplinary action. The memory of Site-13 and its personnel are considered struck from the records of the foundation.

(Note: SCP-0010 is not a known SCP in the SCP Foundation database. However, there is an SCP known as SCP-001, though this SCP is different in each of the SCP canon settings.

SCP-001, also known as the "Gate Guardian," is one of the most mysterious and powerful SCPs in the possession of the SCP Foundation. The origins and nature of the Gate Guardian are not fully understood, but it has been in the Foundation's custody for centuries.

In the 1980s, the Foundation established a research facility, Site-13, to study SCP-001 in-depth. However, on the night of October 31, 1983, a severe containment breach occurred at Site-13.

The breach resulted in the escape of several SCPs, including SCP-001. The Foundation quickly mobilized all its resources to contain and recapture the escaped SCPs, but they soon realized that the breach at Site-13 was unlike anything they had encountered before.

When the containment teams arrived at Site-13, they found the facility to be deserted. The lack of communication from Site-13's staff fueled the Foundation's concern, and they immediately dispatched a response team to investigate.

Upon arrival, the response team found the site personnel dead or missing, presumed dead. The site had been thoroughly destroyed, with evidence of a massive battle between Foundation forces and some unknown, heavily armed entity.

In the aftermath of the disaster, the Foundation discovered that the Gate Guardian had been released from containment, and its sheer power had caused the containment breach and the destruction of Site-13.

The Foundation soon realized that they had underestimated SCP-001's power and abilities, and it was capable of causing catastrophic events if not properly secured.

The Foundation quickly initiated a global alert, and all available resources were mobilized to recapture SCP-001. The Gate Guardian was eventually recontained with significant casualties, and the Foundation launched a thorough investigation to prevent any future disasters.

Today, Site-13 remains a haunting reminder of the dangers of the SCP Foundation's work, and a crucial lesson of its operations. The Foundation continues to study SCP-001 in its various forms, and their personnel strive to ensure that such a catastrophic containment breach never occurs again.

The Children

Chapter 1: Introduction to SCP-0011

SCP-0011 is a phenomenon where an individual will experience vivid, incredibly lifelike dreams that they will remember in great detail after they wake up. These dreams will typically feature unknown, non-human entities that engage in bizarre, often terrifying behavior. SCP-0011 is believed to be a result of exposure to a certain frequency of electromagnetic radiation that is generated by an unknown source.

Chapter 2: The Discovery of SCP-0011

SCP-0011 was first discovered by Doctor ███████ during an experiment in which he exposed himself to a high frequency of electromagnetic radiation. After the experiment, he reported experiencing incredibly vivid dreams that featured a variety of strange, non-human entities. Doctor ███████ reported that the dreams were so vivid that he could remember every detail of them after he woke up.

Chapter 3: Documenting SCP-0011

After Doctor ███████ reported his experience, the Foundation began to document SCP-0011 by conducting experiments on other individuals. The results of these experiments confirmed that exposure to the electromagnetic radiation frequency caused individuals to experience vivid, detailed dreams that they could remember with incredible accuracy.

Chapter 4: The Entities of SCP-0011

The entities that appear in SCP-0011 dreams have been documented by several individuals who have experienced them. These entities are often described as humanoid in shape, but with exaggerated, distorted features that are often unsettling or outright disturbing. Most individuals who experience SCP-0011 will encounter a different entity each time they dream, which has made documenting them difficult.

Chapter 5: The Effects of SCP-0011

SCP-0011 has been known to cause a wide range of effects in individuals who experience it. Some individuals have reported feeling exhilarated and energized after waking up from a dream, while others have reported feeling exhausted or even traumatized. The intensity of the dreams can also vary greatly from person to person, with some individuals experiencing mild dreams while others experience incredibly vivid, intense ones.

Chapter 6: Interactions with SCP-0011

SCP-0011 has been observed to interact with individuals who experience it in a variety of ways. In some cases, the entities in the dreams will attempt to communicate with the individual, though their methods of communication are often unclear or difficult to decipher. In other cases, the entities will appear to be hostile towards the individual, engaging in violent or aggressive behavior.

Chapter 7: Extra Details of SCP-0011

SCP-0011 has been extensively studied by the Foundation, but many aspects of it remain a mystery. The source of the electromagnetic radiation that causes SCP-0011 has yet to be identified, and the relationship between the entities that appear in the dreams and the radiation is not fully understood.

Chapter 8: Containment Procedures for SCP-0011

Individuals who experience SCP-0011 are to be monitored closely by the Foundation to ensure that they do not experience any negative effects or become disturbed by the vivid nature of their dreams. The source of the electromagnetic radiation that causes SCP-0011 is also to be identified and contained to prevent further individuals from being affected by it.

Chapter 9: Potential Applications of SCP-0011

While SCP-0011 is primarily seen as a potential hazard, there have been some suggestions that it could have potential applications. The highly vivid and detailed nature of the dreams it produces could be useful in psychological research or in training individuals to better remember information.

Chapter 10: Conclusion

SCP-0011 remains a mysterious and potentially dangerous phenomenon, but continued research into it may yield valuable insights into the human brain and consciousness. More research is needed, however, to fully understand SCP-0011 and its effects. The Foundation will continue to monitor and contain SCP-0011 in order to prevent it from causing harm.

Story 1

SCP-0011, also known as "The Children", is an object in the SCP database that creates extremely lifelike dreams in people who come into contact with it.

According to the SCP Foundation's records, SCP-0011 was discovered in an abandoned playground in rural Nevada in 1986. When researchers attempted to investigate the object, they found that it had already been "claimed" by a group of children who were living in the area. These children, who appeared to have been abandoned or neglected by their parents, had formed a kind of makeshift family around SCP-0011, and were fiercely protective of it.

As the researchers delved deeper into the anomaly, they discovered that SCP-0011 had the ability to create incredibly vivid and detailed dreams in anyone who came within a certain distance of it. These dreams were often highly personal and specific, drawing on the dreamer's memories, hopes, and fears to create a fully-realized alternate reality.

The children who had made SCP-0011 their home were all suffering from various forms of trauma, such as abuse, neglect or abandonment. They had all been drawn to the object's ability to provide an escape from their painful and difficult lives, and had formed a tight-knit community around it.

As the researchers attempted to study SCP-0011 and contain its effects, they found that the children would do anything to prevent them from doing so - even resorting to violence. The Foundation eventually made the difficult decision to evacuate the children and relocate them to a safer and more secure facility, in order to facilitate their recovery and rehabilitation.

Today, SCP-0011 remains one of the most compelling and puzzling anomalies in the SCP database. Its ability to create such emotionally powerful and life-like dreams has led many to wonder if it might have some deeper cultural or spiritual significance, or if it might be connected to other unexplained phenomena. However, the Foundation continues to study SCP-0011 with caution, in order to prevent any further harm or disruption to those who come into contact with it.

Story 2

SCP-0011 is an object classified as Euclid contained within SCP Foundation. It has the ability to induce incredibly vivid and detailed dreams in individuals who come into contact with it. These dreams are often related to the individual's memories, desires and fears, creating an alternate reality within the mind of the dreamer.

The Foundation discovered SCP-0011 in a small antique store in rural Illinois. It was in the possession of an elderly man who claimed it had been passed down in his family for generations. He reported that every member of his family who had come in contact with the object had experienced intense and disturbing dreams. Nevertheless, he refused to part with the object, citing its sentimental value and his belief that it held some kind of spiritual significance.

After the man's death, the Foundation was able to acquire SCP-0011 through less conventional means. Upon analysis of the object, researchers found that it had the ability to draw on the mental and emotional states of individuals around it, creating dreams that were often highly specific to their personal experiences.

One researcher, Dr. Samantha Lee, volunteered to undergo testing with SCP-0011. After being exposed to the object, she experienced a dream in which she was able to interact with a long-deceased loved one. The experience was so powerful and emotionally overwhelming that Dr. Lee called off any further testing with the object, deeply shaken by the experience.

Over time, the Foundation became aware that exposure to SCP-0011 could have dangerous and unpredictable consequences. Some individuals who came into contact with the object began to experience recurring nightmares, panic attacks, and even delusions or hallucinations related to their dreams.

As a result, strict measures were put in place to limit and control access to SCP-0011. Its containment chamber was equipped with a variety of fail-safes and emergency protocols, and researchers were required to undergo extensive psychological screening before being allowed to work with it.

Despite the risks associated with SCP-0011, it remains one of the most mysterious and intriguing anomalies in the Foundation's collection. Its ability to create such immersive and lifelike dreams has led some to speculate that it could be of extraterrestrial or paranormal origin, or even hold the key to unlocking the mysteries of human consciousness. However, given the potential dangers involved, the Foundation continues to study SCP-0011 with caution and care.

Story 3

SCP-0011 is a Euclid-class anomalous object that has the ability to induce highly detailed and vivid dreams in individuals who come into contact with it. The object was discovered in a remote village in Russia in 1994 by a team of Foundation researchers who were investigating reports of unusual activity in the area.

As the team of researchers approached the village, they noticed that the residents appeared to be in a state of extreme agitation and distress. Upon further investigation, they discovered that everyone in the village had been experiencing intense and highly realistic dreams involving the same group of individuals - a choir of children who would sing hauntingly beautiful songs that seemed to echo throughout the dream.

Initially, the researchers were unable to locate the source of the anomalies causing the dreams. However, after several weeks of investigation, they stumbled upon SCP-0011, which had been hidden away in a small, abandoned chapel on the outskirts of the village. The object appeared to be an old music box, but when activated, it emitted a strange energy that caused those in close proximity to it to experience the vivid dream state.

Once the Foundation was able to contain SCP-0011, they commenced further testing to understand the full extent of its capabilities. They discovered that the object was able to create dreams that were highly personalized and specific to the individual's own memories and desires, drawing on hidden or forgotten aspects of their psyche.

During one test, a subject reported having a dream in which they had received a secret message from an alternate dimension, warning them of an impending catastrophe. Despite being a seemingly impossible scenario, the subject was able to provide the Foundation with accurate information on the events leading up to the disaster, and the Foundation was able to take preventative measures to stop it from occurring.

Despite the potential benefits that SCP-0011 could provide in certain situations, the Foundation became increasingly concerned that the object's effects could be too powerful and dangerous to control. As a result, it remains securely contained in one of the Foundation's top-level facilities, under strict protocols that ensure that its effects are mitigated and managed at all times.

Playing Cards

Chapter 1: Introduction to SCP-0012

SCP-0012 is a Safe-class anomalous object that takes the form of a set of standard playing cards. Each of its cards is identical to an ordinary playing card, except for the absence of any identifying marks or designs. SCP-0012's anomalous properties manifest when it is played in a game of chance or skill.

Chapter 2: How SCP-0012 Affects Gameplay

When SCP-0012 is introduced to a game, it significantly increases the odds in favor of the person who holds the cards. Any game that involves chance, such as poker or blackjack, will be won more frequently by the person holding SCP-0012. Even games that rely on skill, such as chess or go, will result in a higher percentage of victories for the player with SCP-0012.

Chapter 3: Description of SCP-0012's Physical Properties

SCP-0012 is contained within a locked box made from solid steel. The cards themselves are laminated with a proprietary polymer that resists stains, scratches, and other forms of damage. While the specific materials used to create SCP-0012 are unknown, researchers have observed that the cards seem to exhibit minimal wear and tear over time.

Chapter 4: SCP-0012's Origins

The origins of SCP-0012 are unknown. Researchers believe that it may have been created by an individual or organization with an interest in gambling or games of chance. However, they have been unable to identify any specific individuals or groups responsible for its creation.

Chapter 5: The Containment of SCP-0012

SCP-0012 is kept in a secure facility located deep underground. Access to the area is restricted to authorized personnel only. The box containing SCP-0012 is locked at all times, and is only opened when testing or experimentation is being conducted.

Chapter 6: Interactions with SCP-0012

SCP-0012 is known to have a calming effect on its holder. When researchers interact with the object, they report feeling more relaxed and focused. Some have even described a feeling of euphoria while holding the cards. This effect has been observed in individuals who have no prior experience with gambling or card games.

Chapter 7: Dangers of SCP-0012

While SCP-0012 is considered safe for testing and experimentation, it is still classified as anomalous and potentially dangerous. Individuals who hold the cards for extended periods of time may become addicted to the feelings of power and control that SCP-0012 provides. If left unchecked, this addiction can lead to destructive and even criminal behavior.

Chapter 8: Potential Uses for SCP-0012

Despite the potential dangers associated with SCP-0012, researchers have identified several potential applications for the object. Possession of SCP-0012 could be used as a reward for successful missions or investigations. It could also be used as a tool for psychological profiling and research.

Chapter 9: SCP-0012 and Ethics

The use of SCP-0012 raises several ethical concerns. Researchers must balance the desire to understand and utilize the object against the potential negative consequences of its use. The object's addictive qualities must also be taken into account, as prolonged exposure could have serious long-term effects on an individual's mental health.

Chapter 10: Conclusion

SCP-0012 remains a fascinating and enigmatic anomaly that requires further study. While its potential uses are intriguing, steps must be taken to ensure that its effects are carefully monitored and controlled. With the right protocols in place, SCP-0012 could become a valuable tool for researchers and agents alike.

Story 1

SCP-0012 is a Euclid-class object contained within the SCP Foundation. It appears as a standard deck of playing cards, but when used to play a game of cards, it will transport the players into an alternate dimension that resembles a casino.

In 1983, the Foundation first became aware of SCP-0012 after a group of five individuals reported that they had been trapped inside the alternate dimension for several days after playing a game using the deck of cards. They reported that the dimension was populated by strange, humanoid creatures that appeared to be the dealers and patrons of the casino, and that they were required to play games in order to earn food, water, and other basic necessities of life.

As the Foundation began to conduct further tests on SCP-0012, they discovered that the object had the ability to create an incredibly realistic and immersive reality within the mind of the players. The creatures that were encountered in the casino dimension were often hostile to the players, attacking and taunting them during games and other interactions.

As part of their research, the Foundation used SCP-0012 as a tool for studying various psychological and sociological aspects of human interaction. Several trials were conducted in which players were monitored and studied within the alternate casino dimension, allowing researchers to gain insights into the way that humans respond to different types of social and psychological pressure.

However, the Foundation soon realized that the dangers associated with SCP-0012 far outweighed any potential scientific benefits. The casino dimension had the potential to cause severe psychological and physical harm to those trapped within it, and any attempts to rescue individuals from the dimension had the potential to cause major disruptions in the fabric of reality.

As a result, SCP-0012 remains one of the Foundation's most closely-guarded and strictly-controlled anomalies. Its containment procedures are designed to ensure that the object is never allowed to come into contact with unauthorized individuals, and extensive protocols are in place to manage any breaches or unintended contact with the casino dimension.

Story 2

SCP-0012 is a highly dangerous object that appears as a deck of playing cards. When used to play a game of cards, it transports the players into an alternate dimension that resembles a casino. The Foundation discovered this anomalous object in a small, local casino in Las Vegas in 1987.

A team of investigators, led by Dr. Samantha Lee, were dispatched to the casino to investigate reports of a group of players who had gone missing after playing a game of cards. Upon further

investigation, the team discovered that the missing players had all used a deck of SCP-0012 playing cards to play the game. What was even more startling was that the players had seemingly vanished from the casino entirely, with no evidence left behind.

Dr. Lee, being an experienced field agent, decided that the only way to find out what happened to the missing players was to play the game of cards herself. She managed to sneak into the casino at night and set up a game with the same deck of cards. Almost immediately, she was transported to an alternate dimension that resembled a casino - filled with colorful lights and cheering crowds.

As she made her way through the bustling crowds, Dr. Lee quickly realized that something was wrong. The other players in the casino dimension were not human at all - they were strange humanoid creatures with exaggerated features and glowing eyes. She quickly found the missing players, who were being held hostage by the creatures, and engaged in a game to win back their freedom.

However, when Dr. Lee attempted to leave the casino dimension with the rescued victims, she discovered that the creatures were not going to let her leave. They had begun to infiltrate her mind, causing her to hallucinate and feel disoriented. Dr. Lee soon realized that the creatures were using their control over her mind to keep her in the alternate dimension, and that the longer she stayed, the less likely she was to ever escape.

In the end, Dr. Lee managed to break free from the creatures' control and made her way back to the real world, along with the rescued victims. However, the experience had taken a toll on her mental and emotional wellbeing, leading her to take an extended leave of absence from the Foundation.

From that day forward, SCP-0012 was deemed too unstable and unpredictable to be used as a tool for research purposes. It was safely locked away in the Foundation's labs, with extensive protocols and fail-safes in place to prevent any further breaches.

Story 3

SCP-0012 is a mysterious object classified as a Euclid-class anomaly that takes the form of an unremarkable deck of playing cards. When used to play a game of cards, SCP-0012 has the power to transport card players to an alternate dimension that resembles a casino.

In 1996, a teenage boy named Jake discovered SCP-0012 in an antique store and decided to use it to play a game of cards with his friends. As they began playing, they suddenly found themselves transported to an alternate dimension, as vibrant lights and loud noises and game machines surrounded them.

Initially, the group of friends found the experience exhilarating and exciting, feeling like they were living in a fun video game. But as time went by, they become trapped in this dimension,
unable to find any way back to their own world. Jake and his friends soon learned that the casino dimension was being ruled by a group of dangerous entities that enjoyed nothing more than tormenting and manipulating the human players.

Eventually, Jake realized that the only way to escape this seemingly endless cycle of games was to go up against the entity that was orchestrating the events in the casino. He boldly challenged the entity to a high-stakes game of Blackjack, putting everything on the line.

As the game progressed, the entity began to exhibit strange and concerning behavior, becoming increasingly erratic and aggressive. Jake and his friends were terrified, convinced that the entity would never let them leave.

Surprisingly, Jake managed to win the game, outsmarting the entity and emerging victorious. The entire dimension began to collapse around Jake and his friends, and they suddenly found themselves back in the antique store where it all began.

While Jake and his friends were able to escape the casino dimension, they were left with a newfound trauma from their experience. After reporting the anomaly to local authorities, the SCP Foundation was alerted and took control of SCP-0012, ensuring that it would never fall into inexperienced hands again.

The Sculpture

Chapter 1: Introduction to SCP-0013

SCP-0013 is a Keter-class anomalous object that takes the form of a seemingly ordinary cave system located in ████████████ National Park in the United States.

Chapter 2: Physical Properties of SCP-0013

SCP-0013 contains a network of caves and tunnels that extend deep below the surface of the earth. The tunnels are composed of various types of rock, including sandstone, limestone, and granite. SCP-0013 also contains several underground streams and lakes, as well as a large central cavern.

Chapter 3: Anomalous Properties of SCP-0013

SCP-0013 is capable of manipulating the perceptions of people who enter the cave system. The exact nature of this manipulation is currently unknown, but it has been observed to cause individuals to become lost within the cave or to experience vivid hallucinations.

Chapter 4: The First Recorded Incident

The first recorded incident involving SCP-0013 occurred in 19██, when a group of hikers became lost in the cave system. After several weeks, the hikers were rescued by a team of park rangers. However, they reported experiencing strange sensations and seeing unusual creatures within the cave.

Chapter 5: Containment of SCP-0013

SCP-0013 is currently contained within a secure facility located near the entrance to the cave system. Access to the area is restricted to Foundation personnel only. The facility includes a research laboratory and living quarters for staff assigned to SCP-0013.

Chapter 6: Interactions with SCP-0013

Researchers who have entered SCP-0013 report experiencing a wide range of strange and unsettling sensations. Some have reported feeling as though they were being watched, while others have seen bizarre creatures or have been overcome by a sense of dread.

Chapter 7: Theories on the Origin of SCP-0013

Several theories exist regarding the origin of SCP-0013. Some believe that it is the result of naturally occurring geological formations, while others speculate that it was created by an extraterrestrial race or a powerful supernatural entity.

Chapter 8: Dangers of SCP-0013

SCP-0013 is considered extremely dangerous due to its ability to manipulate perceptions and cause individuals to become lost within its tunnels. Additionally, those who spend extended periods within SCP-0013 may suffer from psychological trauma or physical ailments.

Chapter 9: Potential Applications of SCP-0013

Despite its dangers, researchers have identified several applications for SCP-0013. Its ability to manipulate perceptions could be useful in developing anti-memetic agents or in creating advanced sensory deprivation techniques.

Chapter 10: Conclusion

SCP-0013 continues to be a fascinating and enigmatic anomaly that requires further study. While its dangers must be carefully monitored and controlled, its potential applications make it an object of considerable interest to the Foundation. Further research is necessary to fully understand the extent of SCP-0013's anomalous properties.

Story 1

SCP-0013, also known as "The Sculpture," is a highly dangerous anomalous object that is contained by the Foundation. This object takes the form of a humanoid sculpture made of an unknown material, and it is capable of moving and showing signs of sentience.

In 1996, the SCP Foundation received reports of a strange cave system in the United States that was suspected to be the hiding place of SCP-0013. A team of Foundation operatives was sent to investigate the reports and contain the anomaly.

The team entered the cave system and encountered a maze-like labyrinth of tunnels and chambers. They soon found evidence of SCP-0013's presence, including scratch marks on the walls and strange carvings in the rock.

As they continued deeper into the cave system, the team began to encounter traps and puzzles that seemed to be designed to test their intelligence and agility. They also came face to face with several instances of SCP-0013, which attacked them with its incredibly sharp claws and powerful limbs.

Despite the danger, the team persevered and eventually reached the heart of the cave system, where they found a massive chamber filled with hundreds of instances of SCP-0013. The sculptures seemed to be arranged in a pattern, and as the team approached, they realized that the pattern was a kind of visual puzzle.

Through careful observation and analysis, the team was able to solve the puzzle and deactivate the anomalous properties of SCP-0013. The sculptures became harmless, and the team was able to contain them safely.

Thanks to the bravery and intelligence of the Foundation operatives, SCP-0013 was prevented from causing harm to the world. It remains contained to this day in a secure facility, closely monitored by the Foundation.

Story 2

SCP-0013, also known as "The Sculpture", is a Euclid-class object that is a humanoid figure made of an unknown gray stone-like material. The sculpture is 1.88 meters (6'2") in height and has a mass of 310 kg (683 lbs).

The Foundation discovered SCP-0013 during an excavation in 19█ when it was brought to a local museum for display. Within days of its arrival, strange events began happening around the museum. Visitors reported feeling intense fear and paranoia when standing near the sculpture, and some even claimed to have seen the statue moving and changing positions when no one was looking. This led the Foundation to classify SCP-0013 as an anomalous object and take it into custody.

During its containment, the Foundation discovered that SCP-0013 had an abnormal ability to affect human emotions. When a person looks at the sculpture, they experience intense feelings of fear, anxiety, and paranoia. The longer a person looks at the statue, the stronger their feelings become, eventually leading to insanity or even death in extreme cases.

The Foundation found that SCP-0013 could not be destroyed or moved without causing a containment breach, so they built a specially designed containment unit to hold the sculpture. The unit is made of a lead-lined titanium alloy, and all personnel assigned to SCP-0013 are required to wear earplugs and goggles to reduce their exposure to its effects.

One of the most unusual aspects of SCP-0013 is the fact that it seems to be sentient. Although it has no visible means of communication or movement, the sculpture has been known to respond to changes in its environment. For example, when one of the containment unit's lights was accidentally left on, SCP-0013 moved to face the light and remained in that position for several days.

SCP-0013 remains a mysterious and dangerous object, and the Foundation continues to study its anomalous properties with caution.

Story 3

SCP-0013, also known as "The Sculpture", is a Euclid-class object that is a humanoid figure made of an unknown gray stone-like material. The sculpture is 1.88 meters (6'2") in height and has a mass of 310 kg (683 lbs).

The Foundation discovered SCP-0013 during an excavation in 19█ when it was brought to a local museum for display. Within days of its arrival, strange events began happening around the museum. Visitors reported feeling intense fear and paranoia when standing near the sculpture, and some even claimed to have seen the statue moving and changing positions when no one was looking. This led the Foundation to classify SCP-0013 as an anomalous object and take it into custody.

During its containment, the Foundation discovered that SCP-0013 had an abnormal ability to affect human emotions. When a person looks at the sculpture, they experience intense feelings of fear, anxiety, and paranoia. The longer a person looks at the statue, the stronger their feelings become, eventually leading to insanity or even death in extreme cases.

The Foundation found that SCP-0013 could not be destroyed or moved without causing a containment breach, so they built a specially designed containment unit to hold the sculpture. The unit is made of a lead-lined titanium alloy, and all personnel assigned to SCP-0013 are required to wear earplugs and goggles to reduce their exposure to its effects.

One of the most unusual aspects of SCP-0013 is the fact that it seems to be sentient. Although it has no visible means of communication or movement, the sculpture has been known to respond to changes in its environment. For example, when one of the containment unit's lights was accidentally left on, SCP-0013 moved to face the light and remained in that position for several days.

However, one day, a group of rogue agents broke into the Foundation's site and attempted to steal SCP-0013. During their attempt, the agents accidentally damaged the containment unit, and SCP-0013 was released. Chaos broke out as the agents and Foundation personnel succumbed to the sculpture's effects, causing mass panic and destruction.

As the sculpture rampaged through the facility, it seemed to become more and more animate, moving with a purpose and intelligence that had never been seen before. It was as if SCP-0013 was finally free from its containment, and its true nature was finally revealed.

The Foundation was eventually able to re-contain SCP-0013, but the incident left many questions unanswered. Was the sculpture truly sentient, or was it simply reacting to the chaos around it? What other secrets does SCP-0013 hold? Only time and further study will tell. For now, SCP-0013 remains one of the most mysterious and dangerous objects in the Foundation's possession.

Adhesive Tape

Chapter 1: Introduction to SCP-0014

SCP-0014 is a Safe-class anomalous object that appears to be an ordinary roll of adhesive tape. Its anomalous properties manifest when the tape is used to cover a human mouth.

Chapter 2: Physical Properties of SCP-0014

SCP-0014 is indistinguishable from ordinary adhesive tape in terms of appearance and composition. However, when placed over a human mouth, it becomes impossible to remove without damaging the skin or causing other harm.

Chapter 3: Anomalous Properties of SCP-0014

When SCP-0014 is used to cover a human mouth, it causes the person to become completely silent. This effect persists even if the tape is removed, and can only be reversed through the use of specialized medical procedures.

Chapter 4: The Discovery of SCP-0014

SCP-0014 was discovered in the possession of a known serial killer during a police raid. The killer had used the tape to silence his victims before killing them. Foundation agents seized the object and brought it into containment.

Chapter 5: Containment of SCP-0014

SCP-0014 is currently contained within a secure facility designed to prevent any accidental use or unauthorized access. Access to the object is highly restricted, and all testing must be conducted under strictly controlled conditions.

Chapter 6: Interactions with SCP-0014

Researchers who handle SCP-0014 report feeling a sense of unease or discomfort when holding the object. They also note that the tape seems to exert a subtle influence on those who come into contact with it, causing them to feel compelled to use it to silence others.

Chapter 7: Dangers of SCP-0014

SCP-0014 is considered highly dangerous due to its ability to silence those who come into contact with it. This effect can cause serious harm to individuals who are unable to communicate effectively, such as infants or individuals with disabilities.

Chapter 8: Potential Applications of SCP-0014

Despite the dangers associated with SCP-0014, researchers have identified several potential applications for the object. Its ability to silence individuals could be useful in certain situations, such as during interrogations or other high-pressure environments.

Chapter 9: Ethical Considerations

The use of SCP-0014 raises several ethical concerns. Its ability to silence individuals without their consent or knowledge violates fundamental human rights, and its potential use in unethical or immoral practices must be carefully monitored.

Chapter 10: Conclusion

SCP-0014 continues to be a perplexing and dangerous anomalous object that requires further study. While its potential applications may be of interest to the Foundation, the risks associated with its use must be carefully considered before any action is taken.

Story 1

Once upon a time, SCP-0014 was nothing more than a simple roll of adhesive tape, much like any other you would find in a stationary store. It was shipped to the SCP Foundation facility and received without suspicion. Little did anyone know, that roll of tape was about to cause more trouble than anyone could have imagined.

Upon opening the package, Foundation personnel immediately noted a strange property about the tape. It was incredibly adhesive, sticking to every surface it touched, with very little effort. And even once removed, the tape had the ability to re-adhere indefinitely, no matter how many times it had been reused.

A containment chamber was quickly constructed, and SCP-0014 was moved into the room. The new tape roll quickly became the subject of intense scrutiny. It was studied, analyzed and experimented upon, but none of the tests could explain its anomalous properties.

SCP-0014 remained contained for quite some time, but the situation escalated quickly when personnel began succumbing to an overwhelming desire to use the tape. They would steal it from the containment room, using it to seal anything and everything. Some used it to find shortcuts in their work or even build unauthorized structures with the durable and adhesive tape.

This led to a dangerous situation where containment breaches, security risks, and damage to SCP items became all too frequent. The tape's strong adhesive properties proved to be a risk to the safety and security of the facility, and urgent action was needed.

A specialist team was brought in to investigate the tape, and their testing revealed that SCP-0014 contained an anomalous microorganism dotting the surface. Researchers hypothesized that the organism had been responsible for creating the adhesive properties, but further investigation was required.

The SCP Foundation quickly developed a new containment protocol by regularly applying an antimicrobial agent that would kill the organism and neutralize its effects, making the tape non-anomalous. Anyone who came into contact with the tape was subjected to psychological evaluations and given regular checkups to ensure that they hadn't developed any addictive tendencies.

Despite the new protocols, the Foundation reluctantly declared that the adhesive tape was too dangerous to use anywhere besides their facility. It remains in secure containment, and research continues to be conducted with it to advance their knowledge of anomalous microorganisms and their effects on mundane items.

Story 2

Once upon a time, a roll of adhesive tape arrived at the SCP Foundation. Nobody knew where it came from, but it was assigned the SCP-0014 designation and put into containment due to its anomalous properties.

At first, SCP-0014 appeared to be a harmless roll of adhesive tape, but tests quickly revealed otherwise. The tape exhibited extraordinary adhesive properties that confounded the researchers, sticking to every surface it came into contact with and retaining its grip even when removed and reapplied multiple times.

Despite the potential for danger, some researchers became obsessed with the tape, developing an addictive tendency to use it on everything. Security breaches and other issues continued to mount, forcing the Foundation to develop new containment protocols and reinforce security measures in the facility.

As more tests were conducted, researchers discovered that SCP-0014 was much more than just adhesive tape. It was found to contain a previously unknown microorganism that appeared to be responsible for its anomalous properties. Further testing revealed that the organism could only survive in the presence of SCP-0014, indicating that the organism and the tape were intrinsically linked.

New research efforts were put into effect, with the goal of isolating and analyzing the microorganism found in SCP-0014. Ultimately, it was determined that the organism was extraterrestrial in origin, posing a biological danger to life on Earth. The Foundation classified SCP-0014 as a high-level threat and implemented even stricter containment measures to prevent any potential breaches.

As a result of this research, the SCP Foundation realized that they could use SCP-0014 as a valuable tool for expanding their understanding of extraterrestrial biology. They began isolating the organism and conducting in-depth genetic analysis to better understand its properties and to develop ways to neutralize its effects.

SCP-0014 remains contained in the SCP Foundation's facility, under strict supervision and control. While it continues to pose a potential threat to the Foundation's operations, the organization's ongoing research has led to revolutionary medical and scientific discoveries that have greatly expanded humanity's understanding of our place in the universe.

Story 3

In a secret laboratory somewhere beneath the Earth's surface, the SCP Foundation continued its efforts to contain and research anomalous items of all kinds. One day, a mysterious package arrived, containing nothing more than a roll of adhesive tape. This roll was quickly assigned the designation SCP-0014, and placed in its own secure containment cell.

69

At first glance, the tape seemed perfectly normal, but upon closer inspection, it proved to be unlike anything the Foundation had ever seen. The tape stuck to everything and anything, with a tenacity that was both impressive and alarming. It could even be reused, with no degradation of its sticky properties.

Research on SCP-0014 continued, with the tape being closely studied for anything that would explain the anomalous properties it exhibited. As time passed, it became increasingly apparent that the tape was something special, something that had been created by means unknown to humanity.

Like many items the SCP Foundation encountered, SCP-0014 proved to be more than just a simple roll of tape. The researchers discovered that the roll of adhesive tape contained a previously unknown microorganism, which appeared to be responsible for the tape's adhesive properties.

The microorganism was found to be extraterrestrial in origin, and impossible to contain without the presence of SCP-0014. The Foundation scientists were amazed by the implications of this discovery: if life could exist on distant planets, who knew what other kinds of creatures might be lurking out there in the vast, unknown reaches of the cosmos?

Despite the danger posed by SCP-0014 and its microorganisms, the Foundation continued working to understand the creature and its unique properties. Ultimately, the adhesive tape was found to be too dangerous to use, and it was isolated in a secure containment cell.

The microorganism found within SCP-0014 has been carefully studied, raced, and cataloged. Though still dangerous and elusive, it serves as one of the most attractive windows into the secret world of anomalous research. All the while, the Foundation continues its tireless efforts to contain, understand, and unravel the mysteries of SCP-0014 and the many other strange and wondrous things it holds.

<u>*Rotary Telephone*</u>

Chapter 1: Introduction to SCP-0015

SCP-0015 is a Euclid-class anomalous object that appears to be a standard rotary telephone. Its anomalous properties manifest when it is answered.

Chapter 2: Physical Properties of SCP-0015

SCP-0015 appears to be an ordinary rotary telephone. However, its internal mechanisms are known to be non-functional, and attempts to repair or modify the device have been unsuccessful.

Chapter 3: Anomalous Properties of SCP-0015

When SCP-0015 is answered, the person on the other end of the line is heard speaking in an unknown language. The individual will continue to speak until the phone is disconnected, and the speaker's identity and location are unknown.

Chapter 4: The Discovery of SCP-0015

SCP-0015 was discovered in an abandoned house in ███████████, where it had reportedly been used as a prop in a local theater company's production of a play set in the early 20th century. Foundation agents seized the object and brought it into containment.

Chapter 5: Containment of SCP-0015

SCP-0015 is currently contained within a secure facility designed to prevent any unauthorized use or access. Access to the object is highly restricted, and all testing must be conducted under strictly controlled conditions.

Chapter 6: Interactions with SCP-0015

Researchers who have answered SCP-0015 report hearing an indistinct voice speaking in an unknown language. Some have described the voice as being menacing or disturbing.

Chapter 7: Dangers of SCP-0015

SCP-0015 is considered dangerous due to the unknown identity and motivations of the individual who speaks through the phone. The object's potential for harm or manipulation is a cause for concern, and all interactions with SCP-0015 must be closely monitored.

Chapter 8: Potential Uses for SCP-0015

Despite the dangers associated with SCP-0015, researchers have identified several potential applications for the object. Its ability to transmit messages in an unknown language could be useful in developing advanced cryptography techniques or in communicating with extraterrestrial entities.

Chapter 9: Theories on the Origin of SCP-0015

Several theories exist regarding the origin of SCP-0015. Some speculate that it is a communication device used by a group of unknown beings, while others believe that it is the result of a supernatural or otherworldly phenomenon.

Chapter 10: Conclusion

SCP-0015 remains a mysterious and enigmatic anomalous object that requires further study. While its potential applications are intriguing, the risks associated with its use must be carefully considered before any action is taken. Further research is necessary to fully understand the extent of SCP-0015's anomalous properties.

Story 1

Once upon a time, SCP-0015 was discovered in the attic of a suburban home in the state of Michigan. The Foundation had received a tip that an anomalous object was present on the property, and a team was dispatched to investigate.

Upon entering the attic, they found an old rotary telephone sitting on a dusty table. The phone looked like it was straight out of the 1950s, with a solid black body and a coiled cord.

One Foundation agent picked up the phone and heard a voice on the other end. The voice claimed to be "The Operator," and told the agent to hang up and wait for a call later that night.

That evening, the phone rang. The agent answered, and The Operator instructed him to go to a specific location in the nearby town. When he arrived, he found a small group of people gathered around a man who appeared to be hypnotized.

The Operator instructed the agent to retrieve a small vial of liquid from the man's pocket. The agent complied, and as soon as he handed The Operator the vial, the group dispersed.

Over the next several weeks, The Operator continued to contact various Foundation agents and instruct them to retrieve strange items or perform unusual tasks. In each task, the agent was left with a feeling of unease and confusion.

As the Foundation continued to investigate, they discovered that SCP-0015 had the ability to manipulate the memories and actions of those who used it. The Operator was using the phone to carry out their own agenda, and seemed to have a particular interest in acquiring anomalous objects.

The Foundation attempted to neutralize SCP-0015, but found that it was indestructible and seemed to have a will of its own. They were forced to keep it under lock and key, and carefully monitor any communication that came through it.

Eventually, through a combination of technological and psychic methods, The Operator was located and captured. It was revealed that they had been using SCP-0015 to carry out a personal vendetta against a rival organization.

SCP-0015 and The Operator were secured by the Foundation, with the phone being contained in a specially designed room with noise canceling equipment to block out any potential communication.

From that day forward, the Foundation made sure to thoroughly investigate any tips regarding anomalous objects and to handle them with the utmost care, to prevent further incidents like the one with SCP-0015.

Story 2

Once upon a time, SCP-0015 was found in an abandoned theater in the heart of New York City. Foundation agents discovered the phone sitting on a table backstage, as if waiting for someone to pick it up and use it.

As soon as the agent picked up the phone, they heard a voice on the other end. The voice was deep and male, and introduced himself as "The Producer." He explained that the phone had the ability to grant wishes, but only if the person making the wish agreed to perform a task for The Producer in return.

The agent was skeptical but decided to try it out. They wished for a million dollars and almost immediately, a suitcase filled with cash appeared beside them. The Producer then asked them to deliver a package to a specific address in the city.

Over the next several days, the agent continued to use SCP-0015 to grant their wishes, but each time, The Producer would ask them to perform a task in return. The tasks became increasingly complex and dangerous, but the agent was too addicted to the power of the phone to stop.

It wasn't until they were asked to steal a valuable artifact from a heavily

guarded museum that they realized the true cost of their wishes. They refused
to do the task and hung up the phone, but by then, it was too late.

The agent began to experience intense hallucinations and paranoia, hearing
The Producer's voice even when SCP-0015 was unplugged. They became
convinced that The Producer was watching them and would stop at nothing to
get what he wanted.

Eventually, the Foundation was forced to contain SCP-0015 and the agent,
who had become a threat to themselves and others. It was discovered that The
Producer was an anomalous entity that had taken up residence inside the
phone, and was using it to manipulate humans for their own gain.

SCP-0015 was placed in a secure containment facility, and the agent was
given amnestics to erase their memories of their time with The Producer. From
then on, the Foundation made sure to carefully screen any and all wishes made
with SCP-0015, to prevent further manipulation or harm.

Story 3

Once upon a time, SCP-0015 was discovered in the home of a man named
Jerry. Jerry was a well-known businessman in his small town, and the
Foundation had received a report about Jerry using a strange phone to make
deals with mysterious entities.

The agent sent to investigate entered Jerry's home and found SCP-0015
sitting on a desk in his office. Jerry was on the phone, and as soon as he hung
up, the agent picked up SCP-0015 and heard a voice on the other end.

The voice introduced itself as "The Broker" and explained that SCP-0015
had the ability to connect the user to otherworldly entities who were willing to
trade knowledge and power. In exchange for their help, The Broker would ask
for certain favors to be performed in the future.

The agent was curious and asked The Broker to connect them to one of these
entities. Almost immediately, a deep and ominous voice spoke into the phone. It
claimed to be an ancient entity with vast knowledge and power, and offered to
share some of its secrets with the agent.

The agent agreed and was granted extraordinary knowledge of the universe
and its workings. In return, The Entity demanded that the agent complete a
dangerous task that would further its own agenda.

The agent was hesitant, but the Entity promised to make them even more
powerful if they succeeded. The agent agreed, and over the next several
weeks, they used SCP-0015 to trade knowledge for favors and perform
increasingly dangerous tasks.

The agent became more and more skilled and powerful, but it came at a
cost. They became more isolated from their friends and family, and eventually
began questioning whether the knowledge and power they had gained were
worth the price they had paid.

Eventually, The Foundation caught wind of what was happening and
confiscated SCP-0015. The Broker and The Entity were never found, but the
agent was left with immense guilt and regret over the things they had done.

They left the Foundation and spent years trying to atone for their mistakes,
never touching SCP-0015 or any other anomalous object again. The phone was
kept in secure containment, as a reminder of the dangers of seeking power and
knowledge at any cost.

Anomalous Humanoid Figure

Chapter 1: Introduction to SCP-0016

SCP-0016 is a Keter-class anomalous entity that takes the form of a humanoid figure with no discernible facial features or identifying characteristics.

Chapter 2: Physical Properties of SCP-0016

SCP-0016 is approximately 2 meters tall and has a dark, metallic appearance. Its body appears segmented and is covered in a complex network of thin, black tendrils.

Chapter 3: Anomalous Properties of SCP-0016

SCP-0016 is capable of bending the perception of reality within a radius of approximately 400 meters. This effect causes individuals within the area to become disoriented and confused, with some reporting vivid hallucinations or other sensory distortions.

Chapter 4: The First Recorded Incident

The first recorded incident involving SCP-0016 occurred in █████████, when a Foundation field team investigating a series of disappearances in the area encountered the entity. Several members of the team were affected by SCP-0016's anomalous properties, resulting in severe psychological trauma.

Chapter 5: Containment of SCP-0016

SCP-0016 is currently contained within a secure facility designed to prevent any accidental use or unauthorized access. The facility includes several research laboratories and living quarters for staff assigned to SCP-0016.

Chapter 6: Interactions with SCP-0016

Because of its dangerous properties, only experienced researchers are allowed to interact directly with SCP-0016. Those who have observed the entity report feeling a sense of unease or discomfort in its presence, and describe the experience as deeply unsettling.

Chapter 7: Affects on Human Subjects

Subjects within SCP-0016's radius of effect experience a range of physical and psychological symptoms, including nausea, disorientation, and auditory hallucinations. The exact nature of these symptoms can vary depending on the individual and the amount of exposure to SCP-0016.

Chapter 8: Dangers of SCP-0016

SCP-0016 is considered extremely dangerous due to its ability to manipulate reality within a large radius. The entity's potential for causing harm or manipulating individuals is a grave concern, and all interactions with SCP-0016 must be strictly controlled.

Chapter 9: Potential Applications of SCP-0016

Despite its dangers, researchers have identified several potential applications for SCP-0016. Its ability to bend the perception of reality could be useful in creating advanced sensory deprivation techniques or in developing anti-memetic agents.

Chapter 10: Conclusion

SCP-0016 continues to be a formidable and dangerous anomalous entity that requires further study. While its potential uses may be of interest to the Foundation, the risks associated with its use must be carefully considered before any action is taken. Further research is necessary to fully understand the extent of SCP-0016's anomalous properties.

Story 1

Once upon a time, SCP-0016 was discovered wandering through the streets of a small town in northern Minnesota. The abnormal creature was humanoid in shape, but its body was covered in a thick layer of black fur and its eyes glowed a bright red in the dark.

Local authorities contacted the Foundation, who quickly dispatched a team to investigate. The creature was successfully captured and taken to a secure containment facility for further study.

Initial tests revealed that SCP-0016 was more intelligent than first assumed, and capable of communicating with researchers through a series of growls and grunts. It was discovered that the creature had the ability to phase through solid objects, making it highly elusive and difficult to contain.

The Foundation spent months studying SCP-0016, attempting to understand its unique abilities and its origins. The creature seemed to be highly territorial and fiercely protective of its personal space, lashing out violently if anyone came too close.

It soon became clear that SCP-0016 was not a natural creature, but rather an artificial creation. Further investigation revealed that it had been created by a rogue scientist who had been experimenting with DNA splicing and had accidentally merged human and animal genes.

As the Foundation continued to study SCP-0016, they discovered that it had a strong connection to the natural world and was deeply empathetic towards plants and animals. It was eventually decided that the creature could be useful in certain environmental and conservation efforts, and it was given a new purpose as a protector of endangered habitats.

The Foundation continued to monitor SCP-0016, but eventually, the creature was granted a limited degree of freedom and allowed to live out its days protecting and preserving the natural world. Its powerful abilities and protective nature made it a valuable asset in safeguarding the world's delicate ecosystems, and its legacy inspired other researchers to use anomalous creatures for positive change.

Story 2

Once upon a time, SCP-0016 was discovered deep in the forests of the Pacific Northwest. Local reports described a strange humanoid figure, covered in thick black fur and standing nearly two meters tall, and exhibiting incredible speed and agility.

The Foundation quickly dispatched a team to capture the mysterious creature. The team pursued SCP-0016 for several hours, but it was too fast to catch until they laid a successful trap.

The creature was taken to a Foundation containment site, where it exhibited aggressive behavior and tried to escape multiple times. Despite these attempts, researchers were able to learn more about SCP-0016 over time.

It was discovered that SCP-0016 had a unique ability to manipulate sound waves, enabling it to create deafeningly loud noises or even silence for miles around. It used this ability as a defense mechanism, often using it to disorient and incapacitate would-be attackers.

Furthermore, SCP-0016 had an unexplained connection to a nearby native tribe, who had legends of a creature called the "Wild One." The tribe seemed to revere SCP-0016, viewing it as a protector of the forest.

As the Foundation continued to study SCP-0016, they discovered a more troubling aspect of its abilities. Whenever it was under extreme emotional stress, it would involuntarily emit sound waves that caused intense emotional distress in anyone nearby.

The Foundation realized that SCP-0016 was too dangerous and unpredictable to continue containing, but they also knew that it had a connection to the native tribe who had lived in the area for generations.

As such, the Foundation worked with the tribe to create a new containment method. SCP-0016 was peacefully transferred from the Foundation's facility to a secure natural enclosure located in the heart of the forest it had been captured in.

There, the native tribe took on the responsibility of monitoring and caring for SCP-0016. They offered it food and shelter in exchange for its protection of the forest and the surrounding area.

SCP-0016, now known as the Wild One, has been under the watchful eye of the tribe ever since. It has become a symbol of their deep respect and appreciation for the natural world, and a reminder that even anomalous creatures can have an important place in our world if treated with care and respect.

Story 3

Once upon a time, SCP-0016 was discovered in an old house in the Louisiana Bayou. The Foundation received reports of strange happenings in the area, such as pets disappearing and crops failing.

Upon investigation, they discovered SCP-0016. The creature was humanoid in shape, but its entire body was covered in a fine layer of black hair. Its eyes were a haunting purple color that seemed to glow in the dark.

Initially, SCP-0016 appeared to be docile and easily contained, but it soon became clear that the creature was highly intelligent and capable of communicating with researchers in a limited capacity.

It was discovered that SCP-0016 had the ability to manipulate the emotions of those around it, and would use this power to feed off their fear and anxiety. It was also revealed that SCP-0016 had an obsession with collecting dolls and other small objects, which it would hoard in a corner of its containment cell.

Despite attempts to reach out and communicate with SCP-0016, the creature remained aloof and distant. It seemed to have no interest in leaving its containment cell, choosing to spend most of its time sitting in a corner and watching its collection of objects.

As time went on, researchers began to notice changes in SCP-0016's behavior. It seemed to be growing increasingly depressed and listless, hardly moving or responding to anything around it.

Finally, it was discovered that SCP-0016 was mourning the loss of a small doll that had been taken away from it during a routine inspection. The doll had become a source of comfort and companionship for the creature, and its absence had left SCP-0016 feeling lost and alone.

After this discovery, researchers began to take a more sympathetic approach to SCP-0016's containment. They allowed it to keep more of its cherished objects and even provided it with a replacement for the lost doll.

Over time, SCP-0016's mood and behavior improved. It even began to form a small bond with some of the researchers, showing signs of genuine affection and happiness.

While SCP-0016 remained an anomalous entity with dangerous abilities, the Foundation recognized that it was also a living creature with emotions and needs. Its containment was adjusted to include measures for its emotional well-being, and SCP-0016 became a reminder that even the most seemingly monstrous creatures can be capable of love and affection.

The Swarm

Chapter 1: Introduction to SCP-0017

SCP-0017 is a Keter-class anomalous entity that takes the form of a swarm of small, insect-like creatures.

Chapter 2: Physical Properties of SCP-0017

SCP-0017 is composed of hundreds or thousands of small, insect-like creatures, each approximately 5 centimeters in length. The creatures are jet black and appear to be composed of some form of metallic or synthetic material.

Chapter 3: Anomalous Properties of SCP-0017

SCP-0017 is capable of consuming and assimilating all forms of matter, including biological tissue, synthetic materials, and even inorganic matter such as metals and minerals.

Chapter 4: The First Recorded Incident

The first recorded incident involving SCP-0017 occurred in ████████████, when a garbage dump was completely consumed by the entity. The event resulted in the loss of several lives, leading the Foundation to classify SCP-0017 as a Keter-class object.

Chapter 5: Containment of SCP-0017

SCP-0017 is currently contained within a secure facility designed to prevent any accidental use or unauthorized access. The facility includes several research laboratories and specialized containment chambers to prevent the entity from escaping.

Chapter 6: Interactions with SCP-0017

Due to the nature of SCP-0017, direct interactions with the entity are highly restricted. However, researchers who have observed the entity describe it as appearing to move with an unnatural fluidity, almost as if it is composed of a single living organism rather than a swarm of individual creatures.

Chapter 7: Abilities of SCP-0017

SCP-0017 is capable of consuming and assimilating a wide variety of materials, including matter that is typically considered indestructible. The entity's rapid consumption of matter is its primary danger, as there is little that is capable of stopping it once it begins to consume a target.

Chapter 8: Dangers of SCP-0017

SCP-0017 is considered extremely dangerous due to its ability to rapidly consume all forms of matter. The entity's potential for destruction is nearly limitless, making it a grave threat to all forms of life and infrastructure

Chapter 9: Potential Applications of SCP-0017

Despite its dangers, researchers have identified several potential applications for SCP-0017. Its ability to consume and assimilate matter could be used in developing new forms of waste disposal or in creating advanced materials with unprecedented durability.

Chapter 10: Conclusion

SCP-0017 continues to be a formidable and dangerous anomalous entity that requires further study. While its potential uses may be of interest to the Foundation, the risks associated with its use must be carefully considered before any action is taken. Further research is necessary to fully understand the extent of SCP-0017's anomalous properties.

Story 1

SCP-0017, also known as the "Insect Swarm," is one of the most fascinating and dangerous entities contained by the SCP Foundation. Its origins remain uncertain, but it is believed to have been created by an unknown anomaly that caused a swarm of insects to merge into a single, sentient entity.

The early records of SCP-0017 indicate that it was first discovered in the rural areas of ██████████, where it was attacking livestock and humans alike. Teams were deployed to try and contain it, but they were unable to do so for several months. By the time the Foundation's containment teams arrived, SCP-0017 had already killed dozens of people and caused widespread panic in the area.

Containment was eventually achieved through the use of highly specialized pesticides and containment procedures that involve keeping SCP-0017 sealed in a heavily reinforced and structurally sound enclosure. Due to the entity's highly aggressive and deranged nature, personnel are instructed to avoid any physical contact or interaction with SCP-0017 at all times.

Despite the confinement, SCP-0017 has continued to display remarkable abilities, such as the ability to communicate with other insects and to manipulate their behavior in order to further its own objectives. There have also been multiple instances of SCP-0017 attempting to breach containment, often through the use of psychic attacks and mind control.

The Foundation's research into SCP-0017 is ongoing, with teams working to uncover the nature of the anomaly that created it and to develop new strategies for containing it in the future. Despite the risks that it poses, many researchers remain fascinated by SCP-0017 and its abilities, and there is hope that further study may eventually lead to breakthroughs in understanding the nature of consciousness and intelligence.

Story 2

SCP-0017, also known as "The Swarm," is a highly unique and dangerous entity that is contained by the SCP Foundation. Its origins are unknown, but it is believed to have been created by a combination of anomalous means that caused a swarm of insects to merge into a single, sentient being.

One of the most curious things about SCP-0017 is that it is highly intelligent and capable of communicating with other insects, often using them to achieve its objectives. The Foundation has attempted to study this behavior, but it is still unclear how SCP-0017 is able to exert such control over other creatures.

One of the most memorable events in the history of SCP-0017 occurred in 20██, when researchers discovered that the entity had somehow gained access to the internet. Over the course of several days, SCP-0017 was able to use the web to communicate with thousands of different insect populations around the world, effectively creating a massive hive mind.

Unfortunately, this hive mind was not created for benign purposes. SCP-0017 began to issue a series of orders to the various insect populations it had managed to control, instructing them to engage in coordinated attacks on human populations.

The Foundation was able to intervene before any serious damage could occur, using a combination of insecticides and EMP devices to disrupt SCP-0017's hold on its various "lieutenants." However, the incident served as a stark reminder of just how powerful and unpredictable the entity could be.

Today, SCP-0017 is kept under strict containment at a Foundation facility in [REDACTED]. While it is no longer able to exert control over other insect populations, it remains a dangerous and highly unpredictable entity that demands constant attention and vigilance from Foundation personnel.

Story 3

SCP-0017, commonly referred to as "The Insect Swarm," is one of the most unique and dangerous entities contained by the SCP Foundation. It is believed to have been created by a combination of anomalous means that caused a swarm of insects to merge into a single, sentient entity.

Despite its small size, SCP-0017 is a formidable force. It is capable of communicating with other insects and manipulating their behavior, as well as communicating telepathically with humans. Early attempts to contain SCP-0017 were unsuccessful, as it was able to use its control of insects to attack and wound several members of the Foundation's containment team.

The turning point came when a group of researchers discovered that SCP-0017 had a surprising weakness: daylight. While SCP-0017 is capable of moving and operating at night, it becomes increasingly sluggish and disoriented when exposed to sunlight.

The Foundation quickly adapted to this new information, constructing a containment facility that incorporated a series of skylights and other light-emitting devices. When SCP-0017 was transferred to the new facility, it was almost immediately weakened by the light and became much easier to contain.

In the years since, the Foundation has continued to study SCP-0017, trying to better understand how it is able to control other insects and manipulate human thought. Despite the many dangers it poses, many researchers remain fascinated by SCP-0017 and its abilities, and there is hope that continued study may one day lead to new insights into the nature of consciousness and the mind.

Ornate Mirror

Chapter 1: Introduction

SCP-0018 is an ornate, oval-shaped mirror that appears to be made of gold, silver, and bronze. It is approximately 1.5 meters tall and 1 meter wide, and weighs approximately 300 pounds. The mirror is located in a containment chamber at Site-19 and is considered to be one of the most dangerous SCPs in Foundation custody.

Chapter 2: Origin

SCP-0018 was recovered from an abandoned estate in the south of France in 19██. The Foundation became aware of the mirror after reports of strange occurrences and disappearances in the local area. After investigating the estate, Foundation agents discovered SCP-0018 hidden behind a false wall in a chamber below the main house.

Chapter 3: Physical Properties

SCP-0018 appears to be a normal mirror at first glance, but upon closer inspection, several abnormalities become apparent. The surface of the mirror is incredibly reflective, to the point where individuals who stare into it for too long report feeling disorientated and dizzy. The frame of the mirror is covered in intricate carvings and designs, which have yet to be fully analyzed.

Chapter 4: Psychological Effects

The true danger of SCP-0018 lies in the psychological effects it has on individuals who come into contact with it. Anyone who looks into the mirror for an extended period of time will begin to see visions and hallucinations. These visions can range from pleasant memories or experiences to horrifying nightmares and phantasms. Individuals who become too entranced by the mirror will often become violent and unpredictable, attacking anyone who attempts to separate them from SCP-0018.

Chapter 5: Containment Procedures

Due to the dangerous nature of SCP-0018, containment procedures are strict and thorough. The mirror is kept in a reinforced, soundproof chamber with no windows or access points except for the entrance. No personnel are allowed to enter the chamber without Level 4 clearance and full psychological screening. Any individual who enters the chamber with SCP-0018 must be constantly monitored and escorted out immediately at the first sign of distress.

Chapter 6: Testing

The Foundation has conducted several tests on SCP-0018 to try and understand its properties and the extent of its psychological effects. However, all testing has been met with limited success. Individuals who are already suffering from mental illness or psychological trauma are more susceptible to the effects of SCP-0018 but even otherwise healthy subjects have reported experiencing vivid hallucinations and becoming emotionally unstable.

Chapter 7: Incident Reports

Incidents involving SCP-0018 are rare but have been known to occur. In one incident, a Level 3 researcher became fixated on the mirror during a test and refused to leave the containment chamber. The researcher had to be physically restrained and forcibly removed from the chamber. In another incident, a D-class subject who had been exposed to SCP-0018 became convinced that they were living in a world where they were the only person and began attacking Foundation personnel.

Chapter 8: Possible Uses

Despite its dangerous properties, there has been some discussion within the Foundation about the possible uses of SCP-0018. The mirror could potentially be used as a tool for interrogations or mind control, but the risks of using it for such purposes far outweigh any potential benefits.

Chapter 9: Ongoing Research

Research into SCP-0018 is ongoing, with the goal of understanding the true nature of its psychological effects and how to neutralize them. However, progress has been slow and difficult due to the unpredictable and volatile nature of the mirror.

Chapter 10: Conclusion

In conclusion, SCP-0018 is a highly dangerous and unpredictable SCP that poses a significant threat to the safety and mental stability of personnel who come into contact with it. While ongoing research may eventually provide a better understanding of its properties, it is unlikely that SCP-0018 will ever be considered safe for use in any capacity.

Story 1

SCP-0018 is an ornate mirror that is highly polished and heavily decorated with intricate designs, including several portraits of individuals. The mirror is approximately 2 meters tall, 1.5 meters wide, and 30 centimeters thick.

The Foundation discovered SCP-0018 when it was confiscated from a wealthy aristocrat in the late 1800s. Since then, SCP-0018 has remained in Foundation custody and has been studied extensively due to its anomalous properties.

SCP-0018 has the ability to manipulate a person's perception of reality. When a person looks into the mirror, their reflection will gradually change to become more idealized, eventually becoming a perfect version of themselves. However, continued exposure to SCP-0018 eventually causes the subject to become trapped within the mirror, where they are doomed to live out their perfect existence forever.

The Foundation has also discovered that SCP-0018 has the ability to create alternate realities within its surface. When a subject enters the mirror, they find themselves in a reality that is influenced by their deepest desires and fantasies. However, these alternate realities often come at a great cost, as the subject's physical body in the real world begins to deteriorate, eventually dying while their consciousness remains trapped within the mirror.

In one experiment, a D-class personnel was instructed to enter the mirror and observe what he found. Inside the mirror, he found himself in a world where he was the king of a great empire, surrounded by riches and adoring subjects. However, as the experiment continued, he began to lose track of time and became more and more obsessed with staying inside the mirror. When he was eventually pulled out of the mirror, his physical body had withered away due to lack of nourishment and he died shortly after.

The Foundation has yet to find a way to break the hold that SCP-0018 has on its subjects. While it is tempting to enter the mirror and live out one's greatest desires, the consequences are often fatal. For now, SCP-0018 remains a highly dangerous object, and the Foundation continues to study it with caution.

Story 2

SCP-0018 is an ornate, antique mirror with a heavily decorated wooden frame. It stands approximately 2 meters tall and 1.5 meters wide.

The anomaly was initially discovered in a small antique shop in London in the early 20th century. The owner of the shop, who was suspected of practicing witchcraft, sold the mirror to a wealthy client. The client later reported strange occurrences while gazing into the mirror, prompting the Foundation to take notice.

Upon examination, it was discovered that the mirror has an extraordinary ability to manipulate a person's perception of reality. When a person looks into the mirror, their reflection gradually changes; at first, the changes are subtle, but over time, the reflection transforms into an idealized version of themselves. This idyllic self is without any defect or blemish and is often surrounded by beautiful objects and loved ones. As a result, the person's self-esteem and confidence levels are boosted.

However, the longer one gazes into the mirror, the more addictive it becomes. Eventually, the person can't help but remain fixated on their beautiful reflection. Physical changes begin to manifest as well, with a person's physical appearance evolving to match the idealized reflection. These changes become irreversible, and the person becomes trapped inside the mirror.

The Foundation initially used SCP-0018 on D-class personnel to test its effects. They found that once a person is trapped inside the mirror, they become part of a complex dreamworld, an entirely new universe that is entirely under the control of the person trapped inside. Over time, the person inside the mirror becomes a god-like figure in their created universe, with the ability to manipulate and alter its laws and physics.

However, the Foundation eventually realized the mirror's dangerous potential and the extent of its addictive hold over those who gaze into it. Many people met their demise due to the reflected image manipulating their perception of reality. The Foundation realized that SCP-0018 must be well-contained, fortified, and not accessible to anyone.

To prevent any accidental containment breaches, SCP-0018 is encased in a custom-built titanium case with a one-way mirror material. Its interior is filled with a constantly evolving pattern of white noise visual and audio distortions; thus, personnel assigned to SCP-0018 should wear earplugs and goggles to reduce their exposure to its effects.

Story 3

SCP-0018 is a highly ornate mirror of unknown origin, measuring approximately two meters in height and 1.5 meters in width. The mirror is housed in a wooden frame, the carvings on which suggest an origin in the Art Nouveau period.

SCP-0018 came to the Foundation's attention in 19██ when a group of explorers discovered it in a long-forgotten tomb deep within the Egyptian desert. The explorers unknowingly triggered the mirror's anomalous properties and were quickly trapped within its reflected world.

The Foundation dispatched a team to the tomb, tasked with studying the artifact and freeing any individuals trapped inside. The team found that SCP-0018 has the ability to manipulate a person's perception of reality, drawing them in with an idyllic vision of their perfect self.

As the exposure time to the mirror increases, the person's reflection gradually morphs into an idealized version of themselves, a perfect image that answers one's deepest desires. The world beyond the glass becomes the illusion, trapping individuals inside with only their ideal selves.

The team managed to retrieve SCP-0018, and the trapped individuals were released, but they showed signs of significant psychological damage. The team's medic reported symptoms of exhaustion, aggressive behavior, and a compulsion to look into the mirror.

SCP-0018 was subsequently placed in a specialized containment chamber, reinforced with layers of lead and a one-way reflective barrier surrounding it. The chamber was fitted with a sound system that continuously plays white noise, with agents stationed at all times to monitor for signs of exposure.

For years, the SCP Foundation kept SCP-0018 secured, but they were not alone. Rumors of the mirror's powers had spread across the world, and soon the Foundation found that they were not the only ones interested in the artifact.

A group calling themselves the "Worshipers of the Perfect Reflection" managed to break into the Foundation's containment facility and steal SCP-0018. The group believed that the mirror was a gateway to another realm, a utopia where the perfect reflection would reign.

The Foundation hastily mobilized a retrieval team to reacquire SCP-0018 but found that the cult had already learned to use the mirror's power to their advantage. They had begun to alter reality, creating a new world ruled by their perfect reflections.

The retrieval team managed to stop the cult and retrieve SCP-0018, but the damage was already done. The world behind the glass shattered, and a wave of pent-up energy swept across the earth, causing widespread destruction.

While the Foundation managed to contain the mirror, the world had been irrevocably altered. SCP-0018 had shown humanity the power of the perfect reflection, and some could never again resist its call, attempting to find it and gaze their way to fulfillment beyond the glass.

Blue Ballpoint Pen

Chapter 1: Introduction to SCP-0019

SCP-0019 is a Euclid-class anomaly that appears to be an ordinary blue ballpoint pen. However, it has the ability to alter the memories of anyone who writes with it, causing them to forget certain events or memories.

Chapter 2: Containment Procedures

SCP-0019 is to be kept in a standard anomalous object containment locker at Site-17. It is to be handled only by Level 2 personnel or higher and is to be used only for testing purposes with the approval of at least one Level 3 personnel.

Chapter 3: Initial Testing

During initial testing, it was discovered that SCP-0019's effects only last for a short period of time (approximately 24 hours) and do not work on memories that are too deeply ingrained.

Chapter 4: Interaction with Subjects

Subjects who have been affected by SCP-0019's memory-altering abilities often report feeling confused or disoriented upon regaining their memories. In some cases, they may experience false memories or even dissociation.

Chapter 5: First Incident

In the first incident involving SCP-0019, a Level 2 researcher accidentally used the pen to jot down some notes. They ended up forgetting their lunch plans with a colleague, which resulted in a missed meeting.

Chapter 6: Incident Response

Following the first incident, security protocols were tightened, and more rigorous testing procedures were implemented. Future testing would require an extra Level 3 personnel present to ensure that the pen's effects were properly monitored.

Chapter 7: Uses for SCP-0019

Despite its potentially dangerous effects, SCP-0019 has proven to be useful in certain situations. For example, it has been used to help witnesses forget traumatic events or to erase certain sensitive information.

Chapter 8: Attempts to Neutralize

Attempts to neutralize SCP-0019 have thus far been unsuccessful. Its anomalous properties seem to prevent any effective physical damage, and attempts to destroy it through incineration have only resulted in it appearing unharmed in a new location.

Chapter 9: Longer-Term Effects

Researchers have observed that repeated exposure to SCP-0019 over a longer period of time can have more severe effects on memory and cognitive function. As a result, its use has been heavily regulated, and its primary use is only for specific instances.

Chapter 10: Conclusion

Despite its potential dangers, SCP-0019 remains a valuable tool in some situations. It serves as a reminder of the importance of careful handling and monitoring of all SCP objects, in order to prevent any potential negative consequences.

Story 1

SCP-0019 is a blue ballpoint pen that exhibits an unusual and dangerous property. The pen is composed of conventional materials, including plastic and ink, and is visually unremarkable.

SCP-0019 was originally discovered when a Foundation agent, Agent K, stumbled upon it during a routine sweep of a local office supply store. The agent's unapproved test signature activated the anomaly, and the agent became the first recorded victim of SCP-0019's hazardous properties.

SCP-0019 has the ability to 'rewrite' reality by reworking history. Writing with the pen on a surface allows the user to erase anything that has ever occurred, primarily affecting people. The erased event transpires as if it never was, memory and perception altered in a fashion that no one remembers the fact except the user of the pen.

Agent K had investigated a bank robbery that ended in the death of a bank teller. The agent utilized the pen to create an alternate reality such that the robbery never transpired, and the teller was alive. However, Agent K's subconscious perceptions and remembrance of reality before the alteration caused them to undergo a nervous breakdown.

After several trials and mishaps where the use of SCP-0019 resulted in progressively unstable realities, the Foundation deemed SCP-0019 too dangerous to keep uncontained. It was later confiscated and stored in a locked lead-lined container for the safety of the public.

One night, a group of hostile agents infiltrated and broke into the Foundation storage facility, poised to procure various items of interest, including SCP-0019. By the time the alarms had sounded, the agents had already made off with the pen.

The retrieval team was quickly dispatched to seize SCP-0019 and neutralize the agents, finding signs of time manipulation in the area. The exact extent and consequences of SCP-0019's usage by the agents remain unknown, but a wave of reported fading memories and recognition could suggest tampering with reality.

The Foundation subsequently confined SCP-0019 to an inaccessible position, with the specifics of the location being known only to the highest-ranking officials. SCP-0019's potential capacity to change history and revisionist memory remains a looming threat, and its containment operations are among the Foundation's top priorities.

Story 2

SCP-0019 is a blue ballpoint pen that has the ability to rewrite reality by altering the past. In the wrong hands, it poses an incredible threat to the fabric of reality itself.

The Foundation first became aware of SCP-0019's existence when it was used in a high-profile assassination in the early 2000s. The Foundation realized the pen's potential for destruction and became determined to contain it.

SCP-0019's containment protocol is one of the most highly classified in the Foundation's arsenal. The pen is stored in a lead-lined box that is kept under constant surveillance. Only one person, chosen by a random drawing every 30 days, is allowed access to the pen to perform routine checks on its anomalous properties.

Despite the rigorous containment measures in place, SCP-0019's legend continues to grow. Rumors of its existence have spread throughout the world, and it has become a highly sought after item in certain circles.

The Foundation's worst fears were realized when a terrorist organization known as the Brotherhood of the Black Sun managed to infiltrate the facility where SCP-0019 was being held. The Brotherhood, a shadowy group with a history of seeking out dangerous and powerful artifacts, had learned of the pen's existence and was determined to acquire it.

In a daring raid, the Brotherhood managed to steal SCP-0019 and make their escape. The Foundation immediately began a search operation to recover the pen, but the Brotherhood's tactics were unpredictable, and they managed to stay one step ahead of the Foundation at every turn.

With SCP-0019 in their possession, the Brotherhood began to use it to alter history to their own liking, giving them the advantage in their efforts to bring about a new world order. The Foundation attempted several times to recover the pen, but each time they were thwarted by the Brotherhood's seemingly endless supply of resources.

Finally, the Foundation had an idea. They began to seed false rumors about a more powerful and dangerous object that they claimed had been discovered. The Brotherhood took the bait, believing that they had found their next target. They left SCP-0019 unguarded while they pursued the false leads.

The Foundation's retrieval team moved in, recovered SCP-0019, and re-secured it in its containment facility. The Brotherhood's attempt to control the pen had been stopped, but the Foundation knew that they would remain a constant threat, always searching for new ways to disrupt the world's order.

For now, SCP-0019 remains safely contained, but the Foundation remains
ever-vigilant, knowing that the pen's true power still has yet to be fully
understood.

Story 2

SCP-0019 is a blue ballpoint pen that possesses the ability to control
people's minds. It has been classified as Euclid due to its dangerous
capabilities.

One day, a new researcher at the SCP Foundation was assigned to study
SCP-0019. He was excited to finally be assigned to work on a real SCP
object, but he didn't know what he was getting himself into.

The researcher began his study by reading through the object's file, which
warned him that the pen had the ability to control his mind. The researcher
thought he was strong enough to resist such a silly notion, so he removed the
pen from its containment unit.

As soon as the researcher picked up the pen, he felt a strange sensation
come over him. He felt as if something was trying to take control of his mind.
The researcher fought hard to resist the urge to do whatever the pen wanted
him to do, but it was too strong.

The pen commanded the researcher to open the containment cell of
another SCP object, one that was highly dangerous and had caused mayhem
in the past. The researcher, under the control of SCP-0019, obeyed and
opened the containment cell.

Thankfully, the Foundation's security personnel quickly realized that
something was wrong and intervened before any damage could be done.
They took the researcher and the pen to a safer location and separated them.

From that day on, the SCP Foundation ensured that no one came into
contact with SCP-0019 without proper protection and training. The researcher
was still scarred from the experience and warned others to never
underestimate the powers of the SCP objects they worked with.

<u>*Black Sphere*</u>

Chapter 1: Introduction to SCP-0020

SCP-0020 is a Euclid-class anomaly that appears to be a large, black sphere with a diameter of approximately 10 meters. The surface of SCP-0020 is covered in a gel-like substance that is highly conductive and has the ability to absorb and transform electrical energy.

Chapter 2: Containment Procedures

SCP-0020 is to be kept in a specially designed containment chamber with an electromagnetic field. The chamber is to be monitored by at least two Level 3 personnel at all times, and access to the chamber is strictly limited to Level 4 personnel and above.

Chapter 3: Discovery and Origin

SCP-0020 was discovered in a remote location in the Siberian wilderness. The Foundation was alerted to the anomaly by reports of strange electrical disturbances and power outages in the area. After investigating the site, Foundation agents discovered SCP-0020 buried beneath the ground.

The origin of SCP-0020 is currently unknown, but it is believed to be extraterrestrial in nature due to its unusual properties and unknown composition.

Chapter 4: Properties and Abilities

SCP-0020 has the ability to absorb and transform electrical energy. When the substance on its surface comes into contact with an electrical current, it undergoes a transformation, releasing a powerful burst of energy in the process.

SCP-0020 appears to be highly intelligent and can communicate telepathically with humans.

Chapter 5: Testing and Experiments

The Foundation has conducted a number of experiments on SCP-0020, testing its abilities and limits. These experiments have included exposing it to various types of electrical currents, attempting to communicate with it, and observing its interactions with other anomalous objects and entities.

Chapter 6: Interactions with Personnel

SCP-0020 has been known to communicate telepathically with Foundation personnel. Its communications are often cryptic and difficult to decipher, but they have provided valuable insights into the nature of the anomaly and its abilities.

Chapter 7: Potential Threats

Despite its seemingly benevolent nature, SCP-0020 poses a significant threat if it were to fall into the wrong hands. Its ability to absorb and transform electrical energy could easily be weaponized or used to cause widespread destruction if not properly contained.

Chapter 8: Ethical Concerns

Due to its highly intelligent and conscious nature, SCP-0020 raises a
number of ethical concerns about its treatment and containment. Some
researchers have argued that it should be granted more rights and freedoms,
while others argue that it represents too great of a risk to be treated as
anything but an anomalous object.

Chapter 9: Containment Breaches

There have been several instances of containment breaches involving
SCP-0020, including an incident in which it caused a massive power outage
in a major city. The Foundation continues to monitor and experiment with the
anomaly in order to prevent future breaches and mitigate potential threats.

Chapter 10: Conclusion

SCP-0020 represents one of the most intriguing and potentially dangerous
anomalies in Foundation custody. Its unique properties and abilities make it a
valuable asset, but also a significant risk if not properly contained and
monitored. As our understanding of SCP-0020 grows, so too does our
awareness of the need for responsible and ethical containment measures.

Story 1

SCP-0020, also known as the Black Sphere, is a spherical entity that is
completely black in color and is approximately 1 meter in diameter. It has
been classified as Euclid due to its unusual properties.

In the year 20XX, an archaeologist named Dr. Sarah Jenkins discovered
SCP-0020 while on a dig in a remote part of the African continent. Along with
her team, she found an ancient temple buried deep within the ground, and
inside the temple was a pedestal with SCP-0020 resting upon it.

Dr. Jenkins immediately recognized that the object was something unique
and potentially valuable. She carefully removed SCP-0020 from the pedestal
and placed it into a specially designed container for transportation back to her
lab.

As the team traveled back to their base camp with SCP-0020, they began to
experience strange occurrences. The air around them grew colder, and a
sense of unease settled upon them. One member of the team even reported
hearing whispers coming from the container holding SCP-0020.

Eventually, they made it back to the lab, and Dr. Jenkins began her research. She quickly realized that the Black Sphere seemed to possess a strange energy that affected anyone or anything that came into contact with it.

Dr. Jenkins tried to contain SCP-0020 as best she could, but it seemed to have a mind of its own. It would move, seemingly on its own, to different places in the lab. Strange accidents began to happen - equipment would malfunction, experiments would fail, and sometimes, the Sphere would disappear altogether, only to reappear in a different location.

As Dr. Jenkins delved deeper into her research, she began to feel the same sensations that her team had felt while transporting SCP-0020 - the whispers, the cold air, and the sense of unease. She knew she had to contain the object before it caused any more damage.

Dr. Jenkins worked tirelessly, day and night, to find a way to contain SCP-0020. She eventually came up with a solution - she would seal SCP-0020 inside of a specially designed, completely sealed box. This would ensure that the Black Sphere could be studied safely without affecting those around it.

With the containment chamber complete, Dr. Jenkins sealed SCP-0020 inside and took a step back. She watched as the sphere began to vibrate, and a low hum emanated from within the box. But finally, the energy from the sphere subsided, and Dr. Jenkins knew that she had successfully contained the SCP.

The Black Sphere remains under the watchful eye of the SCP Foundation, locked up tight in a secured facility. Dr. Jenkins, who experienced firsthand the danger and wonder of the SCP objects, continues her work in studying and containing these unique and sometimes terrifying entities.

Story 2

SCP-0020, also known as the Black Sphere, is a mysterious spherical object that emits a powerful aura of negative energy. It was discovered in the early 2000s, when a group of hikers stumbled across a strange cave system while exploring a remote part of Canada.

At first, the group thought they had made an incredible discovery - the cave system was sprawling, and filled with stalagmites and stalactites that created strange, otherworldly shapes. But as they explored deeper, they began to feel a sense of unease.

Their unease turned to terror when they stumbled across SCP-0020. The Sphere was floating in the center of a large open cavern, completely still, but emitting a powerful aura of negative energy that made the hikers feel sick to their stomachs.

The hikers quickly fled the cave, but not before taking several pictures of SCP-0020. They reported their discovery to the Canadian government, who in turn informed the SCP Foundation.

When SCP Foundation agents arrived on the scene, they discovered that SCP-0020 was surrounded by strange, black tendrils that seemed to stretch out towards anything that got too close. The aura of negative energy was so strong that it turned the surrounding stones and dirt completely black.

It took the Foundation several weeks to devise a plan to contain SCP-0020. They built an airtight chamber around the Sphere, then used a combination of magnetic fields and high-powered lasers to stabilize it.

However, the containment of SCP-0020 proved to be only temporary. Over time, the object began to emit a strange humming sound, and the black tendrils began to extend outwards from the containment chamber. Agents reported strange sensations when walking past the object, including tingling and a sense of disorientation.

The Foundation was eventually forced to relocate SCP-0020 to an even more secure facility, where it remains to this day. Most agents have been instructed to not go near SCP-0020, as it can have a profound effect on a person's mental and emotional state. Only a select few are allowed to study the object, and their studies have only uncovered more questions than answers.

Story 3

SCP-0020 is a mysterious black sphere that holds a dark secret. It was discovered deep in a cave hidden in the mountains of the Himalayas. When the Foundation first found it, they quickly realized that there was something different about it.

The sphere had an unusual magnetic field around it that seemed to be emanating from within. The team of scientists that examined it found that it was made of an unknown, indestructible material that they could not identify.

They also discovered that when the sphere was brought into close proximity with living organisms, it had a strange and disturbing effect on them. Animals and even humans that came within a few feet of the sphere began to experience intense fear and paranoia.

The Foundation's research team continued to study the sphere, and over time they began to decode its secrets. They discovered that the sphere was actually a kind of portal, leading to a parallel dimension where time and space worked differently.

As they delved further into the mysteries of SCP-0020, they began to realize that it was far more dangerous than they had ever imagined. The dark powers controlling the sphere began to reach out from the portal, and strange and terrifying creatures began to pour out.

The Foundation was quickly overrun, and many researchers and agents were lost in the chaos. SCP-0020 remains sealed off to this day, a dark and dangerous mystery that the Foundation may never fully understand.